LESSONS
from the
CARPENTER

AN **APPRENTICE** LEARNS
FROM **JESUS**

H. MICHAEL BREWER

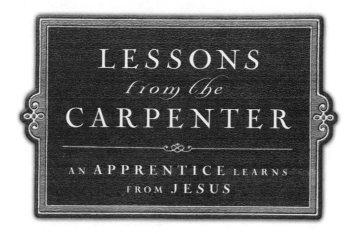

LESSONS
from the
CARPENTER

AN **APPRENTICE** LEARNS
FROM **JESUS**

WATERBROOK
PRESS

LESSONS FROM THE CARPENTER
PUBLISHED BY WATERBROOK PRESS
12265 Oracle Boulevard, Suite 200
Colorado Springs, Colorado 80921
A division of Random House, Inc.

All Scripture quotations, unless otherwise indicated, are taken from the *New Revised Standard Version of the Bible,* copyright © 1989 by the Division of Christian Education of the National Council of the Churches of Christ in the USA. Used by permission. All rights reserved. Scripture quotations marked (KJV) are taken from the *King James Version.* Scripture quotations marked (NIV) are taken from the *Holy Bible, New International Version®.* NIV ®. Copyright © 1973, 1978, 1984 by International Bible Society. Used by permission of Zondervan Publishing House. All rights reserved. Scripture quotations marked (NLT) are taken from the *Holy Bible, New Living Translation,* copyright © 1996. Used by permission of Tyndale House Publishers, Inc., Wheaton, Illinois 60189. All rights reserved.

ISBN: 1-4000-7120-8

Library of Congress Cataloging-in-Publication Data
Brewer, H. Michael, 1954–
Lessons from the Carpenter : an apprentice learns from Jesus / H. Michael Brewer.—1st ed.
    p. cm.
  ISBN 1-4000-7120-8
  1. Jesus Christ—Example. 2. Christian life. I. Title.
BT304.2.B74 2006
232.9'04—dc22

                                                        2005026403

Printed in the United States of America
2006—First Edition

10 9 8 7 6 5 4 3 2 1

For Dad with love (and apologies for the folding rule)

CONTENTS

ACKNOWLEDGMENTS

To Janet—*anam cara*

To Bethany, Rachel, and Kevin—for filling my life with life

To Mom—for Labor Day in July

To Fred and Loretta—for a peaceful place

To Wayne, Dan, and Joe, writers and brothers all

To Cec Murphey—for faith and friendship

To Deidre Knight, agent extraordinaire

To editor Bruce Nygren, man of many boxes, and the good folks at WaterBrook

To Mark—for tapping on the turtle shell

And to John, Ian, Dougie, and friends—for inspiration

LESSONS
from the
CARPENTER

AN **APPRENTICE** LEARNS
FROM **JESUS**

One

JUST A CARPENTER?

"Isn't this the carpenter? Isn't this Mary's son and
the brother of James, Joseph, Judas and Simon?
Aren't his sisters here with us?" And they took
offense at him.

—MARK 6:3, NIV

Isn't this the carpenter?"

That's the question acquaintances and former neighbors
of Jesus posed when he made a brief stop in Nazareth in the
early days of his ministry. The hometown crowd couldn't
swallow the notion that Joseph's boy was passing himself off
as a prophet. The Nazarenes had watched Jesus grow up.

They knew his roots; they daily rubbed shoulders with his brothers and sisters.

The family of Joseph and Mary were nice enough folks, but where did Jesus get the nerve to set himself up as a preacher? He was barely thirty years old, and he was going to tell them about the kingdom of God? Worse yet, Jesus was a workingman. He was no scholar or otherworldly saint but a man who earned his living by sweat and common labor. Whoever heard of a prophet with sawdust in his hair?

"Isn't this the carpenter?"

The insult in those words is unmistakable. How dare this man with callused hands put on airs among his own people! What right had Jesus to speak for God? He hadn't studied at the feet of the great theologians in Jerusalem. He grew up sweeping wood shavings from the floor of his daddy's shop. What could a hammer swinger and saw puller know of the truth? Those bumpkins over in Capernaum might sit at his feet and call him "Rabbi," but the Nazarenes knew better. Joseph's boy could tell stories all day, but that wouldn't change the facts. He was no preacher. He was just a carpenter.

WHY A CARPENTER?

Presumably, the Son of God could have worked at any honest job. Instead of becoming a carpenter, Jesus might just as well have been a weaver or an olive grower. As far as we know, Jesus could have lived among us as a potter or a merchant and still have accomplished his purpose in the world. After all, our salvation depends upon the cross of Christ, not his career. What matters most to us is his life, not his livelihood.

Nevertheless, Jesus's birth in the house of Joseph the carpenter was surely no mere accident, no random event dictated by the shifting winds of fate. God sent the Messiah to a particular family where the boy Jesus would learn the trade of his earthly father.

Why a carpenter? Part of the answer lies in the hard toil of a carpenter's life. The Son of God came to live with us, to be one of us, to share the joys and trials of our daily existence. Had Jesus been born a privileged aristocrat or a wealthy heir, he would not have understood the pressure of earning a living. He would not have known the weary, sweaty labor that is the lot of common people. To meet us where we are, Jesus had to be a worker.

Even so, many jobs of that day demanded physical labor. Fishing the changeable Sea of Galilee, for instance, was both risky and backbreaking. In order to provide flocks with pasture and water, shepherds walked endless miles while battling inclement weather, predators, and loneliness. Farmers struggled to eke crops from stony soil in a dry climate. Any of those jobs would have taught Jesus the meaning of human toil. Indeed, Jesus compared his ministry with each of those occupations—yet none of them quite matches the work of the Messiah:

- A fisherman gathers in the fish just as Christ gathers the lost, but the fisherman doesn't love the fish. They represent a commodity, not a relationship.
- Stained-glass windows depict Jesus as the Good Shepherd, but the picture applies only partially. The shepherd cares for the sheep, calls them by name, and protects them with his very life…so that he may later fleece them and drive them to slaughter.
- In the parable of the sower, Jesus likened himself to a farmer casting seeds in a field. The comparison is apt as far as it goes. A farmer coaxes new life from the seed, but that life flourishes and passes away in a season. A farmer's handiwork is ephemeral, but Jesus built for generations, indeed, for eternity.

LIFE LESSONS IN THE WOOD SHOP

A carpenter builds and repairs. Those tasks comprise the whole craft of carpentry: building what is needed and restoring what is broken. Of all the jobs Jesus of Nazareth might have undertaken, I can imagine no other work that better matches the vocation of the Messiah. As a young Jesus watched Joseph at work in his wood shop, the twin tasks of carpentry shaped the child's view of life and his perception of his calling.

Under Jesus's gaze, Joseph carved ox yokes for harnessing a plow. He hammered together carts and wagons for carrying produce to market. He planed and joined boards into tables and chairs for sustenance and celebration. He built homes for the shelter and nurture of families. With modest tools and the strength of his own hands, Joseph took raw material and created wonders to bless and enhance the lives of his neighbors.

When he did not build from scratch, Joseph redeemed and renewed what was broken. He replaced cracked spokes in wagon wheels. He restored leaky barrels, squared warped doors, and fitted sturdy oak handles to iron ax heads.

Perhaps the young Jesus rode on his father's shoulders when Joseph strode across Nazareth to shore up the sagging roof of a nearby house. Perhaps the boy grew up playing with the curled shavings that rolled from the blade of his father's plane. As Jesus got older, Joseph may have given him small tasks: fetching a tool, marking a line, holding one end of a measuring cord.

According to the custom of that time, somewhere between his thirteenth and fifteenth birthdays, Jesus began formal training in his father's trade. As the Jewish wise men preached, "Teach your son a trade, or you will teach him to steal."

By the time Jesus began his training, he had absorbed many of his father's values:

- Discover the potential within the wood.
- Transform the rough into the useful.
- Meet needs.
- Build to last.
- Never settle for shoddiness.
- Restore whatever can be saved.
- Waste nothing.

The lessons Jesus learned at the carpenter's workbench served him well in later years. His practiced eye recognized the overlooked potential in the human outcasts of society. His skilled touch restored broken spirits and sin-shattered lives. His carpenter's heart decried the squandering of a single life—the loss of even the very least—so he hewed unschooled fishermen into disciples, shaped fallen sinners into witnesses of glory, and hammered embittered persecutors into apostles. And on a dark spring day when he discerned that piecemeal repairs were inadequate to the job, he laid the foundation for a new creation. Like his father, Joseph, Jesus wasted nothing, salvaged whatever could be saved, and built for the future.

WORK THAT MATTERS

God intended Jesus to grow up in a carpentry shop, learning the lessons of a woodworker. This was part of God's plan to mold the mind and heart of the Messiah. Jesus's earthly occupation perfectly mirrored his purpose for coming into the world. Who better to repair a broken creation than a carpenter?

Carpentry is not glamorous work. Nonetheless, after the sweat dries and the fatigue passes, the accomplishment remains. The table serves, the door keeps guard, and the house stands long after the carpenter puts away his tools and moves on to the next job. Whether repairing or building from scratch, a carpenter makes the world a better place.

"Isn't this the carpenter?" sneered the citizens of Nazareth.

Indeed it is, and I take comfort knowing that the Master Builder is the architect of my life and destiny. The one who shapes us for service is a loving craftsman taught from childhood to take pride in his work. The universe at large and our lives in particular are safe and secure in the skilled and callused hands of this Carpenter.

Two

THE MASTER

BUILDER

All things have been created through

him and for him.

—COLOSSIANS 1:16

For twenty-five years of ordained ministry, I have been apprenticed to this Nazarene carpenter named Jesus. I have worked beside the Master Builder while he rebuilds lives, constructs his church, and repairs a broken world. I love the work, and I worship my Boss.

But before I went to work for the Nazarene, I worked for another carpenter: my father. My first job was building houses with my dad. Even as a teenager, I had more of a feel for words than for wood, but Dad was glad to have me at his side because so many tasks in his carpentry business required more than two hands.

Heavy carpentry or framing is no solitary occupation. Partners quickly accomplish jobs that would be difficult for a lone worker: positioning an overhead board, leveling and bracing a wall, chalking a line, even taking a long measurement. Working in tandem also offers the intangible benefit of companionship. Shared work encourages the shared pride of watching a house rise from floor joists to ridge board.

Sometimes, at the end of a long day, Dad and I lingered in the truck, studying a half-built house. Without words we looked upon our common handiwork and saw that it was good. Watching a house take shape through sweat, strength, and knowledge is a joy richer for the sharing.

GOD-AND-SON CONSTRUCTION

Perhaps that explains why the creation of the universe was a Father-and-Son project.

"Long ago God spoke to our ancestors in many and various ways by the prophets, but in these last days he has spoken to us by a Son…*through whom he also created the worlds*" (Hebrews 1:1-2, emphasis added). The Son worked beside the Father, and together they watched the universe take shape. The Father created all things through Christ and for Christ.

Human comparisons pale before the wonder of the partnership between the Father and the Son. Nevertheless, I have an inkling of what that verse means. When I worked with my own father, Dad provided the vision and the guidance for a project, and I helped make that vision a reality. In that sense, whenever I toenailed a stud or laid down a shingle, Dad built *through* me. Every job began with Dad's initiative and energy, and as we worked together, my efforts became an extension of my father's creative will.

On the other hand, construction work was my father's means of providing for his family. Ultimately, my father built all those houses *for* me. Each house was an offering on the altar of love, a willing sacrifice of self-giving.

God has laid all of creation at Christ's feet. In turn, when Christ comes into his reigning power, he will return the redeemed creation to the Father. Not only are you and I—and the rest of the universe—the shared handiwork of the Father and the Son, but we are also the gifts the Father and the Son give to each other from the depths of unfathomable love.

In the beginning the Father ordered all things, and the Son gave form to that order. Together they dug the foundation of existence and poured the footers of creation. Side by side they hoisted the great ridge board of the heavens and shingled the infinite sky with swirling galaxies. With one purpose, Father and Son framed the land and measured the limits of the sea. The Father gave everything to the Son, and the Son offered the universe back to the Father. In joyous communion, Father and Son surveyed their work and saw that it was good.

THE CARPENTER MESSIAH

Human sin and rebellion soon marred God's good creation. Like a family of irresponsible tenants, Adam and Eve and their children vandalized the delicate beauty of God's masterpiece. To put it bluntly, shortly after the human race moved in, the neighborhood went to hell.

A heartbroken God might have written the world off as a total loss, but instead the Father sent his Son, who knew our weaknesses intimately and yet longed to be with us.

I'm reminded of the time my youngest brother was in the market for his first house. He fell in love with a log home on a piece of rugged Tennessee scrubland. When my father inspected the house, he found that some of the walls contained boards cleverly doctored to look like true logs.

"How do you know?" asked the skeptical real-estate agent.

My father's answer was pithy: "I know houses because I build houses."

The Master Carpenter knows us inside and out because he built us. He knows the very blueprint of our hearts. He grasps our possibilities and limits, our dreams and fears. Nothing about us surprises him. He understands how we are made, he accepts us as we are, and he believes in what we can become.

We couldn't fool Christ even if we wanted to. At times in our lives, we may try to disguise the parts of ourselves that we fear will arouse scorn from others. With Christ we can emerge from behind the facade, knowing that the Carpenter accepts "unacceptable" people. The world may condemn us for not achieving someone else's ideal of perfection, but Christ embraces us even with our shortcomings.

My brother bought the log home and lives there today. His eyes were open to its defects, yet he still wanted to be there. Since moving in, he has improved and beautified the building, but he began by loving it just as it was, fake logs and all.

The Master Carpenter recognizes our imperfections, and he still treasures us. He has improvements in mind, but first he loves us as we are.

IN GOD WE TRUST...AND VICE VERSA

Christ also knows our potential. When he created us, he already knew every trial that awaited us. Within the grace of God, no challenge will push you or me beyond our limits.

A friend undergoing chemotherapy and radiation treatments once ruefully told me, "Sometimes I think the Lord overestimates my strength."

Not so! When facing hardships and struggles, we may be tempted to think Christ has forgotten us. Just the opposite is true. Our struggles prove the great trust Christ places in us. He knows our capabilities, and he counts on us to use the gifts he has built into us.

Jesus's disciple Simon Peter learned this on the night before Jesus's death. Peter promised never to forsake Jesus no matter what hardships lay ahead. Jesus knew better, predicting that Peter would deny him three times that very night. But just as the Carpenter understood the frailty of Peter, he also discerned his potential. "When once you have turned back," Jesus said to him, "strengthen your brothers" (Luke

22:32). Jesus was certain that Peter would return to his faith because Jesus knew Peter's "specs." The Carpenter built into Peter sufficient strength to fulfill his calling, just as Christ has built into you and me all the strength we need to remain faithful to him.

Here's another way to look at it: While serving as a counselor in a church camp, I led my campers to the high-ropes course one afternoon. The rowdy boys fell silent as they surveyed the ropes and cables strung between the tall trees. If you've never climbed a high-ropes course, you can't imagine the terror of catwalks and "dead man leaps" thirty feet in the air.

The camp staffer in charge of the course reassured the boys of their complete safety. "Even if you fall," he said, "the safety cable will catch you."

A chubby, freckle-faced boy raised his hand.

"How much weight will those cables hold?" he asked.

"Good question," the leader responded. "The ropes will hold five thousand pounds, the steel cables roughly fourteen thousand pounds. The bolts are even stronger than the cable. This course could carry the weight of a small car."

The freckled doubter eyed the lofty ropes and asked, "How do you know for sure?"

The leader smiled at the anxious camper. Tapping one

thumb against his own chest, the leader said, "I know exactly how strong this course is because I built it."

Christ knows how much you and I can handle because he built us.

LOAD LIMITS

If Christ has constructed us with all the strength we need to live faithfully, why do we fail sometimes? I believe we often encumber ourselves with loads God never meant for us to shoulder.

Even a well-built house can be loaded beyond its limits. Some friends of mine used to live in an older home. They owned thousands of books, and the floor began to sag beneath the weight. Cracks appeared in the walls.

In the basement we positioned steel support posts under the sagging joists. Each post contained a jack, and we heightened the posts until they butted firmly against the joists. At first we raised the posts only enough to stop the sagging of the floor. Over time we elevated the posts very slowly—a fraction of an inch a week—to reverse the decline. Forcing the beams to shift quickly would have been destructive. We added strength to the house slowly so the timbers could adjust to the changes. The reinforcement of the sagging floor represented a partnership of sorts—cooperation between the jacks and the shifting beams.

Christ invites us into a similar partnership. If we are willing to realign our lives with God's plan, he will shore up our sagging strength and fortify us for the day of need. In twenty-five years as a pastor, I have heard this testimony over and over. The words vary, but the substance remains the same. An on-the-wagon alcoholic expressed it this way:

> I could never have gotten sober alone. Every time
> I was ready to give in and reach for a drink, Christ
> gave me enough strength to get through that mo-
> ment. Maybe it came through my sponsor, or I got a
> phone call from a friend at church. Sometimes it was
> something I heard at a meeting or words of Scripture
> that suddenly came alive. There were times I felt
> God's power, and I had no idea how it arrived, as if
> Christ was somehow propping me up. I poured all
> my strength into a bottle, but when I asked for help,
> Christ poured his strength into me.

The Good Carpenter cares about his work, and he earnestly wants you and me to stand firm. Christ builds to last, and he adds strength as needed.

WONDERFUL WORKMANSHIP

So far we have seen that our Carpenter/Creator knows us intimately and loves us just as we are. He built us for victorious living, and he strengthens us when our own resources fall short. But we have yet to explore the most wonderful aspect of our Carpenter's craftsmanship: Christ builds not only for strength; he also builds for beauty.

The Craftsman who invented the intricacies of the atom and painted the startling hues of the peacock also created you and me. He designed us for both beauty and service and shaped us for our own particular places in the world. Each human life bears the hallmarks of Christ's handiwork.

Consider the joyous song of the psalmist: "I praise you, for I am fearfully and wonderfully made" (Psalm 139:14). The works of the Carpenter are wonderful indeed, and we are among those works. We are in awe at the height of mountains, the vast expanse of the ocean, and the orderly motion of the stars, yet we fail to marvel at ourselves.

Make no mistake. You are one of the wonders of the world. You are the handiwork of God. Your very being reflects Christ's craft and skill. He took pride in creating you to be the unique person you are.

When my dad built homes, he added special touches,

such as a longer overhang on the eaves or an extra couple of feet in the floor plan to allow for larger rooms. Most potential buyers never noticed the extras, and I once asked why he invested the additional expense and effort.

"I'm not cut out for mass production," Dad said. "I build a house I'd be willing to live in."

Christ must have felt that way in making you and me. Each of us is a product of loving devotion. Our looks, our gifts, our personalities, even our quirks—all are the handiwork of the Carpenter who takes great pride in his craft.

Jesus builds each human being as if he might end up living in that person.

Three

LOVING

THE WOOD

Let nothing be wasted.
—JOHN 6:12, NIV

Timber was scarce in first-century Israel. Thousands of years of construction, burning, and warfare had diminished Israel's forests. Cypress and cedar grew in the north. Oak and ash were available, though not in abundance. Olive trees grew in the foothills, but the gnarled trunk of the olive is unsuitable for lumber. In New Testament Israel, tall timber trees were scarce. The best wood was imported and expensive.

As a Nazarene carpenter of modest means, Jesus learned to make do. Wood was too precious to waste. A carpenter didn't cut up a long, straight beam for wheel spokes; he set it aside to become a ceiling joist. Planks too rough for a table-top would serve for a watering trough. A bowed piece of oak wouldn't make a doorjamb, but the shape might yield an ox yoke.

The discovery of a fishing boat long submerged in the Sea of Galilee exemplifies this frugality. The vessel, dating roughly from the time of Jesus, contains wood apparently salvaged from junked boats. In fact, the construction is a hodge-podge of different woods: cedar, pine, oak, willow, hawthorn, redbud, and others. The ancient boat builder used whatever was available.

This patchwork boat underscores the preciousness of wood in a deforested country. Waste no scrap! Every odd board must be pressed into service, even to make a boat fit to brave the sudden storms on the Sea of Galilee.

SAVING THE SCRAPS

Modern carpentry places a greater premium on speed than on scrimping, but some craftsmen still approach wood with respect, even reverence. In his garage shop, my friend Pete used to make feeders, birdhouses, brooms, stools, and every conceivable knickknack. Through a connection with a furniture factory, Pete had a sporadic supply of discarded wood in odd shapes and sizes. I once sat with Pete while he sorted a shipment of scraps.

"Here's a piece of mahogany," he said, sniffing it appreciatively before thrusting it under my nose.

"There's a couple of board feet of oak. See those dark flecks in the grain? That's what makes the oak so hard. It'll dull your saw lickety-split. I'll turn that into a cutting board. And what's this?"

Pete gently lifted an almost-black slab from the jumble and cradled it in his thin arms.

"I don't get my hands on ebony very often."

He spoke the word *ebony* as if it were the name of a lifelong friend.

Pete approached a piece of wood in the same spirit the ancient carpenters of Israel did. In a land of scarcity, the artisan befriended the wood. The carpenter's practiced eye studied the length, the shape, the individual flaws. He stroked the grain, considered the heft and texture. Even the smell was a clue as to whether the board was seasoned. With experience and skill, Jesus read the unique story of each board and beam, discovering the best use for each piece and wasting nothing.

Jesus approaches you and me in the same loving manner. Our Lord takes us as he finds us. He lovingly surveys our weaknesses and strengths. He studies the cracks inflicted by sin, the tender places where pain has twisted us. He touches each scar left behind by bitter circumstance or hard choices. Our Savior's discerning gaze lays bare every secret.

Jesus sees what we might have been, the stature we might have attained. No doubt the Carpenter grieves at how far short we have fallen from reaching the glory God desires to reveal in us. If he didn't love us so much, Jesus might well toss us aside in despair or disgust, looking for other timber to better suit his purposes. But he does love us. He loves us as a good carpenter loves the wood. He will not relegate our lives to the scrap heap.

EVERY BOARD IS PRECIOUS

I am a scavenger at heart. When I need supplies for a home project, I rummage through the off-fall at a construction site. Dumpsters are treasure-troves of free lumber and plywood.

Rooting through a scrap heap is undignified, but Jesus didn't cling to his dignity when he clambered down from heaven and entered into the gritty reality of human life. Our Lord climbed into the rubbish of a broken world to rescue us from the scrap pile. He loved us too much to stand by while we went to waste.

In the eyes of Christ, we are infinitely precious, each of us irreplaceable. With nail-scarred hands, he turns us this way and that, peering at every possibility, imagining what beauty and usefulness he might build from our lives.

"I realized I was going to waste," a woman told me at a Christian writers' conference as she recalled her days at a prestigious advertising agency where she knocked down a six-figure income and routinely lunched with media darlings.

"I was using my best talents to sell mouthwash and underwear," she said, "so I took some time off to ponder my life. Although I hadn't been in church for years, I went to a Christian retreat center to think about my priorities. I guess God got hold of me there. I never went back to the agency."

Today she uses her gifts to support causes she believes in. Working with several Christian ministries, she writes a newsletter, a humor column, occasional articles, and copy for brochures.

"I'm not making much money," she says, smiling brightly, "but I'm making a great life."

Christ wants to make something great of you and me. Perhaps we've written ourselves off as scrap. When we look at the raw lumber of our lives, we may see only twisted and broken boards. The Master Carpenter, though, has his own vision of what you and I can become.

Do you remember the story of Jesus feeding thousands of people with a handful of fishes and five loaves of bread? In a miracle of multiplication, Jesus made an abundant meal for the crowd. When the people had eaten their fill, there was still fish and bread left over. Then Jesus did a surprising thing. He instructed the disciples to gather up the leftovers—twelve baskets of uneaten food. "Let nothing be wasted," Jesus told his disciples (John 6:12, NIV).

Why would Jesus bother with the scraps of the meal? He could clearly have made more food, so why be frugal? Because Jesus hates waste! Food is meant for eating, wood for shaping, and people for redeeming. Whatever can be saved should be saved.

HONORING THE GRAIN

Each piece of wood has its own personality. Its flow is known as its grain; a wise woodworker shapes with the grain, not against it.

One of my first building projects was a footstool for seventh-grade shop class. The legs of the stool ended in broad, flat feet. When I assembled all the pieces, the stool wobbled. So I took it apart and used a block plane to trim off the bottom of one of the legs.

At least, that was my strategy. Instead, the plane gouged the wood and chipped off the edge of one leg.

I told the shop teacher, "There's something wrong with this plane."

"No," said the teacher, "there's nothing wrong with your plane; there's something wrong with your plan. Don't plane across the grain. Working against the wood's natural direction tears up the wood."

Turning the maimed footstool leg in his hands, the teacher concluded, "You don't always have to obey the grain, but never ignore it."

A good woodworker savors the personality of the wood and makes use of it. Jesus begins with who we are and plans accordingly. The Master Carpenter doesn't expect you to be someone else. After all, he created you, and he respects the basic grain of who you are. Jesus simply wants you to become the best possible you.

Consider what happened when the Carpenter went to work on the apostle Paul. In his initial encounter with the risen Lord, Paul (then called Saul) was a fanatical Pharisee devoting his whole energy to persecuting Christians and attacking the church. In spite of Paul's hatred for Jesus, the

Carpenter saw amazing potential in this single-minded man from Tarsus. Honoring the grain of Paul's gifts and personality—his learning, his passion for God, his zeal for the truth—Jesus shaped the persecutor into an apostle.

Or think of Simon Peter. When Jesus called Peter to follow him, he didn't ask the fisherman to scrap his old life. Jesus prized the qualities that made Peter a good fisherman: patience, perseverance, intuition, and courage. Jesus invited Peter and his brother, Andrew, to use their fishing skills in a new cause: "Follow me, and I will make you fish for people" (Matthew 4:19). Jesus built on what was there, shaping and forming the old Peter into the new Peter, but always honoring the grain.

Jesus does the same with you and me. He builds with the one-of-a-kind timber of our lives. Whether you are shy or talkative, solemn or fun loving, bold or timid, you are the wood Jesus wants to build with. He can make something spectacular from you, and his work begins with loving you as you are.

I never finished the footstool I began in shop class. My mishap with the plane wasn't my only setback. In trying to round off the stool's edges, I was sloppy with my rasp and dug a deep groove in the wood. The more I sanded and tried to repair the blemish, the deeper it got. I became so disgusted with that scarred, chipped, wobbly footstool that I threw away the whole botched project.

I thank God that our Carpenter never gives up on us! For his own pleasure and glory, Christ made you and me from nothing. Now that we are something, he still works with us, shapes us, builds us. We are unfinished, but our Carpenter has plans for us. The Good Carpenter never abandons his handiwork.

Four

BUILDING ON

BROKENNESS

My grace is sufficient for you, for my power
is made perfect in weakness.

—2 CORINTHIANS 12:9, NIV

An old gospel hymn exhorts, "Give of your best to the
Master." The sentiment is laudable, but we can also
give our worst to the Master. He can use that, too. Jesus is
such a skillful carpenter that he can redeem our twists, burls,
and breaks. Our failures and setbacks, in fact, offer special
opportunities for the Carpenter to shape us for his purpose.

My friend Pete had a collection of billy clubs hanging
over his workbench. He had reserved some of his best scraps

for the lathe and used the spinning tool to carve lengths of wood into ornate table legs or short bats. The billy bats were strictly display pieces, a way to show off striking samples of grain and color. One day Pete pointed out his favorite with a pride usually reserved for photographs of grandchildren.

"See that grain exploding like a starburst? That's burl-wood," he said. "Did God ever make anything prettier than that?"

He looked at me sideways. "You do know what burl-wood is, don't you?"

I confessed my ignorance.

"Sometimes a tree trunk gets a growth or a swelling, like a huge wart or a tumor, maybe two or three feet across. That burl is prized wood. The grain swirls around like cream in your coffee. Furniture makers slice it thin and use it for veneer."

"What causes a burl?" I asked.

"Different things. Could be disease. Or maybe a tree gets hit by a falling limb, and infection sets in. Insects boring into the trunk can also cause a burl. Or sometimes a branch doesn't grow outward the way it should. Instead, the growth turns inward and goes wild, a little like cancer cells. When you see a burl, you know the tree has had a hard time. It's a funny thing, isn't it? A suffering tree makes the most beautiful wood."

Though we yearn for an easy life, hardship can bring beauty to our lives just as it brings beauty to a hurting tree. Struggles temper us. Pain imparts wisdom that cannot be gleaned from books or classrooms. The Carpenter uses even our bitter experiences to build character and compassion into our lives.

STRENGTHENED BY THE STORM

My friend Zoe is writing a workbook on how to recover after a spouse has been unfaithful. She's been sharing this material with small groups for a few years. People listen when she describes the pain of broken promises as well as the possibilities for forgiveness and reconciliation. She's not a trained theologian or a licensed counselor, but she speaks with unmistakable authority because she knows firsthand the betrayal of adultery. Having passed through that particular region of hell, Zoe is eager to help others find their way through.

God didn't cause the adultery that plunged Zoe into anguish, but the Carpenter used that suffering to build her into a person of richer insight, greater compassion, and more far-reaching service. From the burlwood of grief and loss, Christ is shaping a ministry of healing grace.

An adventurer by the name of Tim Severin offers another

example of how we can find strength because of our struggles, not in spite of them. In the mid-1970s, Severin set out to duplicate the legendary voyage of a sixth-century Irish monk who sailed from Ireland to the New World. To follow in the monk's wake, Severin first had to re-create an ancient coracle, a boat made by stretching leather over a wooden frame. Since Severin's life would depend upon the seaworthiness of his boat, he went looking for the best available timber.

A lifelong lumberman advised Severin to use wood from ash trees, especially ash trees that had to struggle for survival on the mountainsides. Scrabbling for life made the wood strong and light. For the mast, the timber master suggested finding a tall, straight ash and taking the wood from the north side of the tree. The north side produces the strongest timber of all, strengthened by decades of raging storms and biting north winds. Life in a sheltered valley provides a tree an easy existence, but the gale-battered face of a mountain grows the strongest wood.

POWER FROM WEAKNESS

Finding strength in struggle and blessing in brokenness is the mystery behind Paul's words to the Christians in Rome: "We know that all things work together for good for those who love God, who are called according to his purpose" (Romans 8:28). We relish the gentle summers of growth when the timber of our lives stretches out straight and proud, but the skill of Christ redeems even storm-ravaged, sick, and broken lives.

The apostle Paul experienced this firsthand. Even after his dramatic conversion, he found it difficult to believe that the Carpenter can build on our weaknesses. Some years after becoming a Christian, Paul prayed fervently for Jesus to take away a damaged piece of his life, what Paul called the thorn in his flesh (see 2 Corinthians 12:6-9). We don't know what that thorn was. Some have guessed epilepsy or a disease of the eyes or recurring depression. Whatever it was, he hated it.

In fact, calling Paul's affliction a thorn understates the extent of his misery. The Greek word Paul used for "thorn" actually refers to a wooden stake or a sharpened picket used to build fences on a battlefield. Being pierced by a thorn scarcely compares to being impaled on a stake. The apostle suffered terribly from his burden. He called it a messenger from Satan.

Paul twice prayed for healing but received no answer. Only after Paul's third appeal did the Carpenter reveal his will: "My grace is sufficient for you," Christ told Paul, "for my power is made perfect in weakness" (2 Corinthians 12:9, NIV). In the eyes of Christ, the apostle's so-called flaw was a means of displaying God's boundless power and love. Jesus wanted people to look at Paul and say, "If God can do so much with a broken person like that, surely God can use me, too."

Sagging Houses Wanted

Before my parents fully retired, they spent several years buying unwanted, dilapidated houses and turning them into showplaces. The more run-down the house, the more eager they were to renovate it. The before-and-after contrast amazed the neighbors. When added to hard work, know-how and creativity can give new life to a broken-down house.

Of course, my parents brought to their remodeling business one other crucial gift: vision. Where others saw a shack, my parents saw potential. They enjoyed defying the proverbial wisdom that "you can't make a silk purse from a sow's ear." They even printed business cards, dubbing themselves "Silk Purse Remodeling."

In just this way, Christ claims and reclaims us. He knows what to do with ramshackle lives and dilapidated people. "For surely I know the plans I have for you, says the LORD, plans for your welfare and not for harm, to give you a future with hope" (Jeremiah 29:11). Someone has observed that every saint has a past and every sinner a future. Even though we are sometimes frail and run-down, the Carpenter can use our weaknesses to create something beautiful—a rebuilt life established on a foundation of hope.

Five

SHAPING

THE WOOD

If your hand or your foot causes you to stumble,
cut it off and throw it away.

—MATTHEW 18:8

In the Greek language of the New Testament, Jesus is
called a *tekton*. That word is usually translated "carpenter," but the same word can also be applied to blacksmiths
and stone carvers. A more faithful translation of *tekton* might
be "shaper." In his career Jesus was a shaper of wood; in his
ministry, Jesus is a shaper of people.

We have seen that Jesus shapes us lovingly, respecting

even twisted and knotted wood. But now we must accept another essential truth of carpentry. When carpenters shape wood, they do so by cutting. Now, these truths remain:

- Jesus loves us without conditions.
- Jesus accepts us—knots, cracks, and all.
- Jesus begins with us as we are.

Nevertheless, Jesus intends to cut away from our lives the parts that interfere with his plan for us.

THE KINDEST CUT

How else can a carpenter shape wood except by cutting? The craftsman may use a saw, an ax, an adz, a plane, a drill, or a chisel. Perhaps the removal of a portion of the wood is so slight that a rasp or file will suffice. Whatever the means, the result is the same. The carpenter creates by hewing away all that does not serve the intended purpose.

In this regard, carpentry differs from other crafts. The potter shapes clay by pressing and squeezing. The blacksmith shapes iron by heating and hammering. The silversmith uses crucibles and molds. Fabric can be folded and pleated; leather can be stretched; glass can be poured or blown. Lumber defies those shaping techniques. Wood can't be melted, pounded, or molded. With rare exceptions, the only way to shape a board is by hewing, hacking, sawing, chopping, or rasping anything that stands in the way of the wood's destiny.

Christ sometimes used vivid language and shocking images to catch the attention of his listeners. Perhaps no saying of Jesus disturbs us more than the passage in which our Lord applied this basic principle of carpentry to his disciples:

> If your hand or your foot causes you to stumble, cut it off and throw it away; it is better for you to enter life maimed or lame than to have two hands or two feet and to be thrown into the eternal fire. And if your eye causes you to stumble, tear it out and throw it away; it is better for you to enter life with one eye than to have two eyes and to be thrown into the hell of fire. (Matthew 18:8-9)

Jesus is speaking figuratively when he charges us to cut off hands and feet and pluck out eyes for the sake of the kingdom, but his intention is unmistakable. If the Carpenter is to shape us according to his divine blueprint, we must relinquish anything that undermines his design.

An everlasting destiny awaits, and no sacrifice is too great in the fulfillment of that plan. Our Carpenter is not building for the decades or even the centuries. The pyramids of Egypt represent a weekend project compared to the work Christ has undertaken in us. He is shaping us for eternity.

DEAD WEIGHT

When Christ saws away the harmful excess from our lives, our hearts may ache and throb. Like Job, we may cry out to God, "Your hands fashioned and made me; and now you turn and destroy me" (Job 10:8). Jesus, however, will remove nothing that belongs to our true and best selves. He will carve away only the things that prevent us from becoming the persons God intends.

I knew a fellow named James who went from four hundred pounds down to two hundred. Physically speaking, James lost half of himself, yet he has not diminished as a person. At minus two hundred pounds, he is healthier and happier. Now he can do things he couldn't before, such as tying his own shoes. He has a richer, fuller life because he shed excess pounds that had no rightful place in his life. Losing that two hundred pounds was the hardest thing James has ever done. Do you think he regrets it? Do you suppose he misses that weight? Nor will we miss the things Christ carves from our lives, because he takes away only what doesn't belong.

Sometimes less is more. Wood lore teaches that cutting

away a piece of wood may create a stronger board. Occasionally the rafters in old barns display shallow notches where carpenters in colonial America chiseled out knots on the underside of the beams. They believed that knots created weak spots and encouraged cracks.

What Christ chisels from our lives invariably makes us stronger:

- the anger that smolders in our hearts and flares into hateful words or vicious criticism
- the self-condemnation that whispers in the quiet corners of our minds
- workaholism and insatiable perfectionism
- enslavement to drugs, alcohol, lust, greed, or food
- the shame and unhealed wounds of an abusive upbringing
- the guilt of family secrets, repressed wounds, and unconfessed sins

When Paul encountered Christ, Jesus cut away a great deal that was not part of Paul's eternal destiny: his adherence to the Law of Moses, his theological certainties, his Pharisaic pride, his position in the Jewish community, his passionate hatred for Christians. All this and much more Paul gave up so that he might be shaped according to the plan of Christ.

Did Paul regret his losses? Writing to his friends in the Philippian church, he said,

I once thought all these things were so very important,
but now I consider them worthless because of what
Christ has done. Yes, everything else is worthless when
compared with the priceless gain of knowing Christ
Jesus my Lord. I have discarded everything else, counting it all as garbage, so that I may have Christ and
become one with him. (Philippians 3:7-9, NLT)

Paul didn't grieve for the things Christ took away. No,
he would have gladly surrendered a thousand times more in
order to feel the Carpenter's smoothing touch on his rough
and splintered life.

Our Carpenter has a vision of what we were meant to be
and can yet become. He distinguishes between the needful
and the harmful. Even when we cling to the very things that
cripple us, he knows what must be taken away to reveal our
true nature and to shape us for our upward calling. He hews
away every false love so that we may find our heart's true desire.

Giving All to Receive All

We need withhold no aspect of our battered lives from the
restoring touch of the Carpenter. Above all else, Christ wants
our heartwood. A tree's heartwood isn't necessarily stronger

than the sapwood, nor does it always have better color or grain. The heartwood is simply the living core of the tree, the center around which all else grows. Whatever we may offer to our Carpenter, if we withhold our heartwood—the innermost core of ourselves—then Christ's work is hampered.

Christ expects nothing less than everything from his followers. All we are, all we know, all we can be—this is what Christ asks from us. Of course, this sounds as if we'll end up keeping nothing. Worse yet, it sounds as if we'll end up *being* nothing. But the opposite is true: The more we give ourselves to Christ, the more we become.

Peter once asked Jesus about this. He said to Jesus,

> "Look, we have left everything and followed you."
> Jesus said, "Truly I tell you, there is no one who has
> left house or brothers or sisters or mother or father or
> children or fields, for my sake and for the sake of the
> good news, who will not receive a hundredfold now
> in this age…and in the age to come eternal life."
> (Mark 10:28-30)

Home, family, and livelihood. Jesus names the very things we harbor in our heartwood. He promises that when we surrender our deepest self to his shaping, we will receive a hundred times more in return. Jesus is talking not only about the distant rewards of heaven but also about rewards in this world and this age, rewards of growth, fulfillment, personal worth, and service. This is the great adventure of laying ourselves in the hands of the Master Carpenter, grain and gifts, burls and scars, heartwood and all.

LOVE'S CHISEL

The Presbyterian Historical Foundation in Montreat, North Carolina, displays a wonderful exhibit of woodcarvings in the lobby. Using mostly local walnut, retired minister John Mack Walker has carved various scenes from the life of Christ. The carver depicts Jesus and his disciples in the work clothes and rough boots of the Appalachian mountaineers.

I have never seen Walker at work, but I can imagine the process. Before the carver is a rough block of walnut. He sees in that wood something no one else can see—a beauty to uncover, a truth to reveal. He chips away all that does not belong to his vision. With mallet and chisel, he cuts off the unwanted growth. The vision takes shape piecemeal until Christ is revealed from within the wood.

You and I were made in the image of God. We are meant to look like Christ. Nothing that obscures God's image belongs in our lives, so the Carpenter cuts from you and me everything that doesn't look like God.

For those who have never yielded themselves to the Carpenter, this surely appears to be a kind of dying. Yet the loving chisel of the Carpenter makes more of us, not less. His handiwork is not our destruction but our salvation.

Six

JOINING
THE WOOD

On that day you will know that I am in my
Father, and you in me, and I in you.
—JOHN 14:20

Carpentry requires two fundamental skills: shaping
wood and joining wood. Any carpenter who can't put
two pieces of wood together and make them stay is in the
wrong business. While nails may be our first choice for joining boards, nailing isn't always the best option. Not only are
nails unattractive for finish work, but they sometimes split
the wood and often work loose over time.

Jesus used nails in his work, but perhaps sparingly. Hand-forged iron nails were expensive at the time. Fortunately, a skilled craftsman of his day had other options. A joint often worked better than a nail, just as it does today. Jesus likely used some of the various joints that woodworkers still employ, such as dowel joints, lap joints, dadoes, rabbets, tongue and groove, mortise and tenon, dovetails.

No doubt, Joseph learned joinery from his father and passed it on to Jesus as part of his stock in trade. One needn't be a furniture builder to grasp the essential principle of joinery: For two boards to interlock, they must be shaped to fit each other.

Resting in Each Other

This practice of interlocking boards in a joint explains a puzzling New Testament idea. The Bible teaches that we dwell in Christ and that Christ also dwells in us—a notion contrary to common sense. We may put a box into a bag, or we may put the bag into the box, but they cannot simultaneously be inside each other.

The teaching goes back to Jesus himself: "On that day you will know that I am in my Father, and you in me, and I in you" (John 14:20). Theologians resort to convoluted metaphysics to make sense of this, but the likely answer is much simpler. When Jesus said, "I am in you and you are in me," perhaps he was speaking as a carpenter. When two boards are fitted together in a joint, one abides in the other.

A dovetail joint offers a good example. Woodworkers began using this style of joint centuries before Jesus. The carpenter notches the ends of two boards and fits the notches together like interlacing fingers. When this joint is executed well, the boards interlock securely, each one resting in the other.

Our Lord shapes us so that we are fitted and fastened to him. We are joined to Christ and Christ to us, connected to form an interlocking and enduring joint. We are never again alone, never forsaken, never abandoned, never lost. We may shoulder a cross, but we no longer bear that burden by our strength alone. We may walk a hard road, but not by ourselves. If we weep through sleepless nights, another heart beats in time with ours in the darkness. When we rejoice, Christ's joy is added to our own. When we are at peace, Christ's peace permeates ours. In all our living, the abundant life of Christ fills us.

When he wrote to the Roman Christians, Paul wondered aloud whether any power is strong enough to sever the connection between Christ and his people:

> For I am convinced that neither death, nor life, nor
> angels, nor rulers, nor things present, nor things to
> come, nor powers, nor height, nor depth, nor any-
> thing else in all creation, will be able to separate us
> from the love of God in Christ Jesus our Lord.
> (Romans 8:38-39)

What can separate us from Christ? No power above or below, nothing that is or ever will be, nothing in the whole vast universe of God's creation! When Christ joins us to himself, we are joined inseparably.

A GOOD FIT

A strong joint requires a snug fit. Each board must be shaped to fit the other precisely. Christ made the first move to create this fit between himself and us when he laid aside his omnipotence as the Son of God and became human. To join us in our humanity, Christ shaped himself in our image. He came to earth in our likeness to make a snug fit.

The Son of God exchanged eternal glory for hunger, sweat, blisters, fatigue, and mortality. The Christ whom the whole universe could not contain willingly became a microscopic cluster of cells in the womb of a teenager. The one through whom all things were created became himself a creature, shivering in a stable and crying for milk. Why this immeasurable descent from heaven? So that God's Son might fit his life into ours.

For a joint to be strong, though, we must be shaped into Christ's likeness as well. This shaping happens over time. We grow better fitted to Christ because the Holy Spirit works within us. We cannot make ourselves into the image of Christ; only the Holy Spirit can do that. But we can cooperate with the process.

By way of comparison, consider pregnancy. The conception of a baby is a gift, and the woman who carries that new life does not control the gift. The new life grows at its own pace and in its own way. Yet the woman who wants to encourage that new life will practice certain habits (such as eating well and resting sufficiently) and spurn others (such as drinking alcohol and smoking).

So it is with Christians joined to Christ. Our Lord plants a new life in you and me, the abundant life of Christ dwelling in us. That new life is a gift that is beyond our control, but we can partner with that indwelling life as it grows in us. Faithful habits of prayer, studying the Bible, and developing Christian friendships open us to the influence of the Spirit. The more the Spirit shapes us to fit our Lord, the stronger the joint through which Christ abides in us and we abide in Christ.

STRONG GLUE

What else makes a joint secure? Strong glue. In the first century, carpenter's glue was made from an animal by-product called collagen. Woodworkers today have their favorite glues and may reject any glue but their preferred brand. The general dictum is this: Use the best glue you can find. Preparing a well-fitted joint is careful, precise work. After so much effort, it's not worth it to scrimp on the glue.

What is the best glue to strengthen our union with Christ? Like woodworkers, Christians have different options. Faith is excellent. So is obedience. Trust carries a lot of weight. But surely love is the best glue of all. "God is love, and those who abide in love abide in God, and God abides in them" (1 John 4:16).

Love cements the joint. In strengthening our connection with Christ, nothing we can do is more important than loving our Lord with heart, soul, mind, and strength.

We may probe the depths of theologies and unravel great mysteries. We may move mountains and work wonders. We may raise funds to build cathedrals, hospitals, and schools.

We may lead great reform movements. But without love, all this means nothing and comes to nothing. Unless we love Christ, our Christianity is hollow.

The heart clings fast to what it loves. The more we love Christ, the tighter the connection we have with him.

STRENGTH THROUGH STRESS

What else can we do to strengthen our connection with Jesus? A carpenter knows that every joint is subject to stress. Shear stress, for instance, is the tendency for two boards to slide across each other. Tensional stress tugs boards in opposite directions. But compressional stress, which presses boards together, can be useful to a carpenter. The savvy woodworker harnesses compressional stress to strengthen a joint.

Suppose we're building a bookcase. We've constructed the frame. We're going to put in shelves that will be under considerable stress when books are piled on them. How do we keep the shelves from shearing out of place? One solution is to cut grooves on the inside of the bookcase and slide the shelves into those grooves, creating a dado joint. The beauty of the dado is that added weight only presses the shelf more firmly into place. This is one way to use compressional stress.

Stress is unavoidable in our lives. Discipleship doesn't

exempt us from problems and burdens, but we have a choice as to how we will handle those difficulties. Sometimes we allow problems to drive a wedge between our Lord and us. Disappointment turns into bitterness. Doubt undermines trust. Impatience begets anger, and the gulf between us widens.

I know a man who hasn't been in church since his wife died years ago. Her death was a hard, painful passing. He prayed frantically for her, and when physical healing wasn't granted, he buried his faith along with his wife. The pain drove him away from the Christ he once loved.

Oddly enough, I'm acquainted with another man who never had time for God while his wife lived. He sat in the parking lot waiting impatiently for her to emerge from worship or choir practice. After her death, he entered the church building for the first time in years. His grief drew him into a relationship with Christ.

Grief can build one person's faith and break another's. Helplessness may lead to despair or to trust. Hardship can cause us to push Christ away, or it can propel us into his arms. When God's face is hidden, some people decide there is no God, while others learn to believe in spite of the darkness. God can transform even the most painful disappointments for our benefit if we persevere in loving him in spite of our setbacks. In the midst of heartbreaking anguish, a friend of mine confessed the kind of faith that builds strength upon stress. "I have discovered," he said to me, "that even when God cannot be understood, he can still be trusted."

THE WEIGHT OF LOVE

We needn't be ashamed when we get angry with God. The psalms are replete with indignant prayers accusing God of breaking promises and ignoring needs. Such psalms remind us that even when we hurl accusations at heaven, we are still in relationship with God. If we seize the sleeve of Christ and yell, "How dare you do this to me!" at least we are still hanging on to Jesus. That attitude—the determination to remain connected to God even if we don't like God much at that moment—makes the difference between a strong joint and a weak one.

The Old Testament character Job lost everything he cherished: health, children, money, and reputation. Although bitter and bewildered, he refused to let go of God. Broken, sick, impoverished, and bereaved, Job still vowed through clenched teeth, "Though he slay me, yet will I hope in him" (Job 13:15, NIV).

Dig deeply to the core of your being where you make the most fundamental decisions, that place where absolute values are shaped. Find the cornerstone of your faith, and there on the foundation carve these three words: "No matter what!" If we can engrave on our hearts, "I am with Christ no matter what," then grief, pain, and loss will not separate us from him. The stress will bring us closer to Christ. The weight will strengthen our ties instead of weakening them.

If this seems too much to ask, I can only point you to the Cross as a reminder that when God asks for our commitment in spite of suffering, he isn't asking us for anything more than he was willing to give. Through his crucifixion, Jesus made the ultimate connection that joins us to him in grace. He dreaded the Cross and asked God to find another way to accomplish our salvation. Yet when the time came, Jesus accepted the way of *sacrifice* and paid the ultimate price so that we might be reunited with God.

From what we know of the Roman practice of crucifixion, Jesus didn't drag the entire cross through the streets of Jerusalem; he carried only the horizontal beam. The uprights remained permanently in place at the execution grounds. When the condemned criminal arrived, he was nailed to the horizontal beam and then hoisted to a place where a notch on the crossbeam slid into a matching notch on the upright post. Those notches came together in a solid carpenter's joint. A dowel or peg may have reinforced the connection, but the primary strength of the joint depended upon the weight of the convicted man to seat the connection with compressional stress.

With the weight of his dying body, Jesus made the joint that held the cross together.

With his terrible death, our Savior cemented the connection that joins us to him.

Love is truly the strongest glue.

Seven

UNDER CONSTRUCTION

Which of you, intending to build a tower, does not first sit down and estimate the cost, to see whether he has enough to complete it? Otherwise, when he has laid a foundation and is not able to finish, all who see it will begin to ridicule him, saying, "This fellow began to build and was not able to finish."

—LUKE 14:28-30

Any carpenter who wants to remain in business must learn to estimate costs. He also needs to make sure that he has available whatever materials are needed to see the job through to the end. Jesus was no exception. Even in a job as simple as carving an ox yoke, Jesus had to know the cost of materials and the required hours of labor before quoting a price. If he miscalculated the cost or labor, he could lose money on the project. Just as today, on a large job the potential loss could be devastating.

We envision Jesus puttering on wagon wheels and benches in his modest woodworking shop, but he may have participated in much grander building projects. The sizable city of Sepphoris rose three miles from Jesus's home in Nazareth. The city had been sacked and burned within a few years of Jesus's birth, but Herod Antipas adopted the ruins as a pet project. He invested decades rebuilding the city as a Roman cultural center. Jesus grew up almost in the shadow of that impressive building program. We wouldn't be stretching the facts to suppose that Joseph and his eldest son occasionally supplemented the family income with jobs in the nearby city where carpenters were in great demand.

COUNTING THE COST

The proximity of the cosmopolitan city to Nazareth may explain why Jesus mentioned a tower—an uncommon sight in rural life—in one of his parables. When Jesus compared the undertaking of discipleship to the construction of a tower, he may have been recalling some contractor's ill-considered work in Sepphoris.

> For which of you, intending to build a tower, does
> not first sit down and estimate the cost, to see whether
> he has enough to complete it? Otherwise, when he
> has laid a foundation and is not able to finish, all who
> see it will begin to ridicule him, saying, "This fellow
> began to build and was not able to finish." (Luke
> 14:28-30)

Jesus's words about counting the cost are exactly what we would expect from a seasoned carpenter. What more public embarrassment presents itself than an unfinished building falling into ruin? Every passerby would laugh derisively at a builder who undertook a job he couldn't complete.

Jesus didn't want to discourage potential disciples, but he insisted that would-be followers consider the cost of obedience. The Carpenter seeks disciples who will not only make a good beginning but will endure to the end.

Yet the parable of the unfinished tower is more than a cautionary story. It also implies a promise of help. Surely Jesus himself counted the cost before undertaking our redemption. The Master Carpenter would not promise us salvation if he could not complete the job. Every Christian is a work in progress, and Christ will see that work through to the end.

We need not fear the outcome of our salvation unless we believe that Christ has overextended himself. Could this be true? Has the Carpenter underestimated the cost of our personal salvation and abandoned the job? Our progress in discipleship often feels painfully slow. Might our Lord walk away from you or me and turn his hand to some more promising project?

THE DEEPEST POCKET

To answer this question honestly, we must first consider what prevents a carpenter from finishing a job. One of the most common reasons that buildings are not completed is that the builder ran out of money.

For instance, an embarrassing monument to overenthusiasm sits on Calton Hill overlooking the charming city of Edinburgh, Scotland. The national monument was intended as a memorial chapel in honor of those who died in the Napoleonic Wars, but funding was inadequate for the grandiose scheme. Amid great fanfare, the builders laid a cornerstone and erected twelve massive pillars—and promptly ran out of money. More than 150 years later, the proposed church remains unfinished. The purposeless pillars loom on the skyline as a constant reminder of dashed hopes.

Could Jesus fall prey to the same folly? Might the Master Carpenter abandon our salvation because he lacks the resources to complete what he has begun in our lives? The New Testament rejects the possibility, repeatedly bearing witness to the immeasurable resources of Christ.

To reassure the Ephesian Christians, for example, Paul wrote that we have redemption in Christ "according to the riches of his grace that he lavished on us" (Ephesians 1:7-8). Far from confessing a shortage of grace, the apostle insisted that "the power at work within us is able to accomplish abundantly far more than all we can ask or imagine" (Ephesians 3:20).

God's grace abounds far beyond our needs. The Carpenter working on you and me has not only counted the cost; he has already paid the full price.

THE ETERNAL BLUEPRINT

Poor planning might also derail a construction project. Years ago a construction company contracted with my father to build a trilevel home for a client. The house was well underway when the client visited to review the progress. As he walked through the house, he complained that the rooms were not laid out correctly. Everything in the house was out of place. Even the elevation of the three floors was out of kilter. My father verified the construction according to the blueprints, but the man insisted that this wasn't the house he had asked for.

He was absolutely right. The company had given my father the wrong plans. The house my father was building had almost nothing in common with the house the man wanted. To fulfill the contract, the company paid my father to rebuild the house from scratch, even pouring a new foundation. If not for a possible lawsuit, the company might have abandoned the job, leaving behind a botched and unfinished house that nobody wanted.

Could this happen to Jesus? Is the Master Carpenter working from the wrong plans? In explaining his lifework, Jesus said,

> For I have come down from heaven, not to do my
> own will, but the will of him who sent me. And this
> is the will of him who sent me, that I should lose
> nothing of all that he has given me, but raise it up
> on the last day. (John 6:38-39)

In a few words, Jesus reminds us that he is faithfully carrying out God's blueprint in all things.

God worked out a blueprint for our destiny before the world began. The names of those who belong to Christ have "been written from the foundation of the world in the book of life of the Lamb" (Revelation 13:8). Much of God's plan remains hidden from us, but we don't need to read the blueprints. We need only believe that God's purpose for us is eternally secure and that Christ will fulfill that plan for our future glory.

FAULTLESS WORKMANSHIP

One other problem might prevent the completion of a building project: poor workmanship.

A few years ago my friends moved into a brand-new home, but their excitement dimmed when they found their "finished" house riddled with problems: jammed windows, dead outlets, doors that wouldn't close, switches wired to the wrong lights, a leaky dishwasher, and a toilet that filled with hot water after every flush.

Shoddy workmanship accounted for the long list of mistakes. The builders didn't care about the house, and the quality of their work unmasked their indifference. A hireling does what is required to receive the day's wages, but a professional takes pride in the finished product.

Christ is proud of his work in our lives. He builds not for pay or praise but for the joy of pleasing his Father. Christ will present nothing less than his best to God. The Good Carpenter will never cut corners or disguise shabby work. Redeeming the world is more than a job; it is the Son's eternal offering of love to the Father.

A redeemed and restored universe laid at the feet of God may be more than we can imagine, so let's put a personal face on the scene. Not only will the Carpenter offer a renewed creation to God, but he will lead you and me to God's throne as well.

Christ will present us to God holy and blameless, without a single fault—no second-rate craftsmanship, hidden flaws, or unfinished work. Christ makes us the people we were meant to be, and each of us who has allowed the Carpenter access to our lives will find our faith vindicated as Christ completes his work in us. When we approach God, the Carpenter will stand beside us to vouch for his work, proud of completing God's plan for our lives.

Lesser builders might leave a job unfinished because the project is too costly, the plans are too confused, or the work is too demanding. An incompetent worker might walk away from a half-finished tower. Not the Master Carpenter. He knows the plan. He loves the work. And no price is too high to rebuild a broken man or woman who is precious to God. We may be unshakably confident of this: "He who began a good work in you will carry it on to completion until the day of Christ Jesus" (Philippians 1:6, NIV).

What this Carpenter begins, he also finishes.

Eight

THE SOLID
FOUNDATION

The rain fell, the floods came, and the winds
blew and beat on that house, but it did not fall,
because it had been founded on rock.

—MATTHEW 7:25

For several years I served on the board of a children's home in mountainous eastern Kentucky. The director's home perched upon a steep hillside overlooking the campus. Problems plagued that house: persistent leaks, cracked walls, jammed windows and doors, and dripping pipes. The reason for this endless parade of repairs? The house was sliding down the hillside.

Built cheaply, the house lacked a proper foundation. Rather than digging to the bedrock, the builders constructed the house upon the soil of the mountain slope. The eye couldn't detect the house's downhill movement, but gravity was prevailing. Every minute shift of the foundation resulted in cracked plaster, separated shingles, and leaky plumbing. We bulldozed the house and rebuilt from scratch, this time in a different location.

FACING THE FLOOD

Jesus the carpenter taught that a reliable foundation is crucial for both raising a house and building a life. On at least two occasions, Jesus illustrated this idea in stories. The more familiar version of the parable provides the finale for the Sermon on the Mount.

> Everyone then who hears these words of mine and
> acts on them will be like a wise man who built his
> house on rock. The rain fell, the floods came, and the
> winds blew and beat on that house, but it did not
> fall, because it had been founded on rock. And every-
> one who hears these words of mine and does not act
> on them will be like a foolish man who built his

house on sand. The rain fell, and the floods came,
and the winds blew and beat against that house, and
it fell—and great was its fall! (Matthew 7:24-27)

The terrain of ancient Israel presented challenges in home construction. Building a house in a valley was simple and straightforward. Centuries of wind and rain had leveled the lowlands with sand and gravel washed from the hills.

Building on high ground posed a more difficult challenge. The bare rock of the hills served as a foundation, but the solid stone might have to be leveled. Even if a naturally flat shelf was available, the builder still had to lug materials uphill, and the homeowner might have to haul water as well.

Many opted for the easier course. Houses on the valley floor served well as long as the weather was agreeable. In that dry environment, a house built on the sand might stand secure for generations—until a heavy storm struck. Deep snowfall in the mountains, coupled with an early thaw and unusually heavy rains, would send torrential floods raging through valleys. Within hours a trickling stream could become roaring white water.

Such floods were brief but fierce. Speaking of a house built on the sand, Jesus said, "The rain fell, and the floods came, and the winds blew and beat against that house, and it fell—and great was its fall!" On the other hand, the house built high upon the rock stood firm while floods ravaged the valley below.

A HOUSE ON HIGH GROUND

This story admonishes us to choose a stable place upon which to build our lives. Our culture offers us endless acres of tempting building sites: wealth, career, reputation, hedonism. We needn't be ashamed of making money or excelling in our work or enjoying healthy pleasures, but none of these passions offers adequate ground upon which to build a life secure from storms. Jesus's parable points our way to safer ground.

Reminding his Corinthian friends of where they had placed their faith, Paul wrote, "For no one can lay any foundation other than the one that has been laid; that foundation is Jesus Christ" (1 Corinthians 3:11). If we establish ourselves upon any ground other than Christ, we are building upon shifting sand. In a flood, unreliable ground gives way. A different outcome awaits the life built upon Christ. Faith does not spare us the storms of life, but the believer remains standing after floodwaters subside.

When my daughters were young, we used to build towers from wooden blocks, making the stack as tall as possible. Every time we tried to build our tower on the tabletop, someone shook the table and the blocks tumbled. To make the game last more than two turns, we built on the hardwood floor. Even jumping up and down—a tactic we tried from time to time—would not topple the tower on the firm, solid floor.

Jesus is the only unshakable foundation. Building elsewhere invites trouble. No other ground upholds us to the end and beyond.

THE ROCK BENEATH THE SAND

We have considered the foundation parable as recorded in Matthew's gospel. Luke's gospel presents a different form of the story. In this version Jesus takes us back to the broad, sandy valley, but he adds a twist in the tale.

> I will show you what someone is like who comes to
> me, hears my words, and acts on them. That one is
> like a man building a house, who dug deeply and laid
> the foundation on rock; when a flood arose, the river
> burst against that house but could not shake it, be-
> cause it had been well built. But the one who hears

and does not act is like a man who built a house on
the ground without a foundation. When the river
burst against it, immediately it fell, and great was the
ruin of that house. (Luke 6:47-49)

Matthew emphasized choosing the right place to build,
but Luke shifted the focus away from location. Instead, he
focused on digging deeply to build the best possible house on
the firmest foundation, even in a risky place. Both home-
owners built on the flat, dry ground. When the flood came,
the torrent swept away only the house that lacked a foundation. The other house was equally battered, but that builder
excavated through the sand to the bedrock. With a foundation established on rock, the house survived the flood.

Matthew's version of the parable reminds us to choose
wisely as we establish our lives. But Luke's version acknowl-
edges that we aren't always free to choose our situation. In
Luke's gospel, Jesus stressed the need for a firm, deep
foundation, even when we find ourselves in undesirable
circumstances.

What if we end up in a place we never meant to be?
Maybe we have been victimized by the choices of other
people or by events we couldn't control. Many times we find
ourselves in situations we didn't choose. A family is in finan-

cial straits, the husband laid off six times in the past three years by corporate whim. A woman with three young children is suddenly single. She doesn't believe in divorce, but her ex-husband does. A man suffers permanent, chronic pain after a collision with a drunk driver. A woman invests years preparing for the career of her dreams, only to have her vocation rendered obsolete by advancing technology just as she graduates.

We don't always get to choose our circumstances, but beneath hateful situations is bedrock we can build upon if we delve deeply enough to uncover the healing foundation of Christ. A friend of mine, for instance, longed for motherhood but could not have children. Her faith unshaken, she offered the painful disappointment to Christ. She trusted his goodness and waited for his plans to unfold.

As it turned out, the quietness of a home without children allowed my friend to develop a rich, contemplative spirituality, a wellspring that blesses her and those around her. That spiritual depth in turn nurtures her work with Big Sisters, an organization that provides mentors for youngsters who need a feminine adult presence. I doubt that all the grief has evaporated from my friend's heart, but upon the foundation of Christ, she has built a rewarding, worthwhile life. If we fix our future on Christ, the present cannot undo us.

BUILDING THE BEST FROM THE WORST

The watery city of Venice is an engineering marvel, but that's not why it was built as it was. The city fathers built on the lagoon only because they had no other choice. No doubt they would have preferred to erect a proud city on dry, solid ground, but repeated invasions drove them out to the scattered islands in the lagoon. Adapting to life on the water was a dire necessity.

The Venetians made the best of their desperate circumstances. With no solid ground available, they made their own. They drove tree trunks into the sandy mud like giant fence posts, placing them snugly side by side so that the tops of the trunks created a level surface. The builders then topped the wooden pilings with a thick layer of limestone. This provided the foundation necessary for erecting buildings. At first the people remained on the marshy islands, but these determined builders later expanded upon the shallow floor of the lagoon.

Although born of hardship and struggle, Venice became a cultural center of art and commerce. No one would willingly elect to build soaring cathedrals upon the muddy ooze of the sea bottom, but the Venetians established a strong foundation in the worst of circumstances.

Each of us can point to conditions in life that we didn't

choose and never desired—physical disability, recurring depression, marital strife, career setbacks, illness, bankruptcy—yet these frustrations need not define our limits. With the help of the Master Carpenter, we can build lives of beauty, wonder, and accomplishment in even the most unpromising situations.

Carpenters know that the foundation limits the building, determining the size and scope of the structure. The building cannot be wider than its foundation; even the height of a building depends on how much weight the foundation can bear. In life we are limited not so much by our unchosen circumstances as by our chosen foundation. If we build upon the rock of Christ, what can curtail our growth? No burden is too heavy to bear when Christ upholds us. No God-given aspiration is too lofty if we stand on the Rock of Ages. In a world beset by painful and tragic limitations, Christ is the foundation without limits.

A story from the life of Aleksandr Solzhenitsyn, the Russian author and historian, is a beautiful illustration of this. Solzhenitsyn spent many years in a brutal Siberian work camp, surviving the days in a haze of dehumanizing labor and abuse. One afternoon he felt he could go on no longer. Why continue to live in such a terrible place? Dropping his shovel from blistered hands, he slumped onto a bench. He waited for a guard to order him back to work. His refusal would lead the guard to beat him to death as an example to others. Solzhenitsyn had seen other prisoners suffer the same fate, and now he numbly awaited the only escape available to him.

But as he sat on the bench, another prisoner approached. A bent and scrawny old man knelt before the bench. Without uttering a word, the emaciated man scratched a crude cross in the dirt at Solzhenitsyn's feet and then returned to his work. Solzhenitsyn stared at the cross, first in perplexity and then with growing wonder.

In the cross Solzhenitsyn recognized something more powerful than the Soviet Empire, more enduring than evil, a reality beyond the bleak misery of his suffering. Those two lines in the dirt held out the promise of redemption and dignity even on the doorstep of hell. He rose slowly, retrieved his shovel, and went back to work. His outward circumstances had not changed, but inwardly the prisoner had dug deeply enough to find a worthy foundation for life.

A PLACE TO STAND

Through the gospel parables, the Good Carpenter teaches us two foundational truths. Jesus urges us to choose carefully where we will build our lives. His teachings offer us high ground—acting on his word ensures spiritual security. That's the first fundamental truth.

And when faced with circumstances we would not have chosen, we may emulate the man who dug deeply through the soft, sandy soil to lay a firm foundation in a poor location. Upon a solid base, that house withstood the flood. That's the second foundational truth: In even the worst of circumstances, we may establish our lives upon the bedrock of Christ.

Archimedes, the ancient Greek thinker and mathematician, once said, "Give me a place to stand, and I shall move the world." The Carpenter provides a solid place to stand. Whether or not we move the world, when we take our stand on Christ, the world will not move us.

Nine

THE MOST IMPORTANT STONE

See, I am laying in Zion a stone, a cornerstone
chosen and precious; and whoever believes in him
will not be put to shame.

—1 PETER 2:6

Hymns, sermons, and stained-glass windows rarely depict one of the most prominent biblical symbols representing Jesus. To explain his mission, Jesus appropriated a carpentry term rooted in Israel's prophecies of the coming Savior. While teaching in the temple, he asked, "Have you never read in the scriptures: 'The stone that the builders rejected has become the *cornerstone;* this was the Lord's doing, and it is amazing in our eyes'?" (Matthew 21:42, emphasis added).

THE STONE OF TURNING

No fewer than seven times the writers of the New Testament referred to Jesus as a building stone. We tend to think of Jesus as a woodworker, but recall that the Greek word usually translated "carpenter" in the New Testament can apply to stonemasons as well. In an age before specialization, a small-town carpenter cultivated a range of skills, including basic masonry.

The Old Testament phrase that compares Jesus to a stone literally means "stone of turning." That term indicates the crucial block laid where a rank of stones turns the corner and begins a new wall. What is not clear in Hebrew is where this stone of turning is located.

In English we call the foundation stone at the juncture between two walls a *cornerstone.* The top stone that ties two walls together and completes the block laying is called a *capstone.* English translations of the Bible usually refer to Jesus as the cornerstone, but either meaning applies to Christ equally well. He is the cornerstone (the beginning of the work), and he is also the capstone (the completion of the work). All things begin in Christ, and in Christ all things find fulfillment.

Even if you've never laid a single stone or brick, this biblical teaching is easy to grasp. Masonry begins with the cornerstone. If the cornerstone is inadequate in size, shape, or placement, the building will suffer. On the other hand, if that stone is properly positioned and secure, the walls will align correctly, resulting in a solid, sturdy building.

Once, while hiking in the Scottish Highlands, I visited a crofter's cottage that embodied this rule of solid construction. This stone house stood on a steep slope, but a massive boulder projected from the lowest corner of the foundation, securing the entire structure on the hillside. In houses of this design that are built upon a grade, the cornerstone is sometimes carefully placed; at other times the house is situated to take advantage of a naturally jutting boulder that serves as the cornerstone. In either case, the massive stone anchors the foundation and walls. The whole house rests upon the strength and stability of that cornerstone.

Christ offers himself as our cornerstone, in effect saying, "What begins with me begins well. If you ignore my guidance and calling, your life will be out of kilter. Put me at the threshold of your life, at the head of your goals and dreams, and I will help you build a life both sound and secure."

BUILDING UPON THE BEGINNING

Yet a good beginning must be followed by faithful progress. What the cornerstone begins, the capstone completes. Life in Christ requires growth. The letter to the Hebrews hints at God's impatience with those who begin a good work in Christ but never follow through. The writer challenges Christians who are in a comfortable rut to resume building lives that glorify Christ: "Let us go on toward perfection, leaving behind the basic teaching about Christ, and not laying again the foundation" (Hebrews 6:1).

The Hebrew Christians had the right foundational beliefs but failed to apply those beliefs in daily life. After laying a foundation, they took a permanent coffee break. The writer urged them to progress toward perfection rather than resting on past efforts.

In New Testament Greek, the word translated "perfection" suggests completion, something that is fully finished. In essence the writer of Hebrews said, "You've started with a good, solid foundation in Christ. For heaven's sake, now build something on it!"

Taken together, the cornerstone and the capstone suggest the fullness of the Christian life, both founded on Christ and continually building toward Christ.

WALLS AT WAR

What happens if the cornerstone fails or the capstone slips? Cracks appear. The walls pull apart at the corners and lean away from each other. If the turning stone fails, the house faces disaster. This is the catastrophe Jesus had in mind when he said, "If a house is divided against itself, that house will not be able to stand" (Mark 3:25). Jesus drew a carpenter's picture of inward division—a house doomed to fall because its walls are out of kilter with one another.

I saw a house in Israel afflicted with this problem. The structure was built of stones cemented together by mud mortar and then plastered—usually a durable style of construction in a sun-scorched land. Near one corner, though, a crack ran through the front wall from the roof to the ground. The crevice at the top of the wall was large enough for me to poke my arm through. One wall leaned perilously.

Either the cornerstone was out of line or the builder had failed to tie the walls together at the capstone. Rather than wait for the walls to topple, the owners wisely abandoned their tottering home. A house so seriously divided against itself couldn't be salvaged; it could only be destroyed. In time, gravity would provide the demolition.

Through this carpentry image, Jesus offers a sober

warning about the danger of double-mindedness. In the long run, a divided life is likely to collapse under its own weight. Making decisions based on the teachings of Jesus safeguards us from the tension cracks of mixed loyalties. If drawing nearer to Christ is our guiding principle, we avoid tottering in two directions at once. The remedy for a divided existence is trusting Christ to be our cornerstone and capstone—the motivation for our deeds and the goal of our aspirations.

WORTHY OR WORTHLESS?

The ancient Jewish rabbis told a parable about the building of the Jerusalem temple in the days of King Solomon. According to the story, the builders repeatedly passed over one particular stone. Mason after mason picked up this stone, considered it for a place in the walls, then tossed it aside as not quite right.

When the time came to finish the walls of the temple, the workers searched frantically for the perfect capstone to complete the building. Eventually they returned to the discarded stone and discovered that it was the perfect shape. That despised stone crowned the temple and held the whole construction together.

The rabbis claimed that this was the story behind the

lines in Psalm 118: "The stone that the builders rejected has become the chief cornerstone. This is the LORD's doing; it is marvelous in our eyes" (verses 22-23).

This is the very verse Jesus quoted to describe his own ministry. As the Carpenter traveled through Israel, some rejected him while others left everything to follow him. Jesus inspired both enmity and friendship, but he rarely encountered indifference.

One might imagine Jesus as a rock in the path. Some trust the stone to bear their weight and help them along the path; others trip over it. But no one can ignore the stone. As Paul put it, "See, I am laying in Zion a stone that will make people stumble, a rock that will make them fall, and whoever believes in him will not be put to shame" (Romans 9:33).

TRUSTING THE KEYSTONE

The Hebrew expression for "stone of turning" carries one more possible meaning. The carefully shaped stone at the top of an arch where the curving angles meet is called the *keystone*. The name reveals the stone's importance; it is the key to the strength of the whole arch. If the keystone is strong and well fitted, the arch is secure. If not, the arch collapses under its own weight.

Legend depicts an ancient king who worried that the royal builders might do shoddy work in constructing his palace. On the day the workers finished, while the scaffolds and supports still braced the stonework, the king came to inspect the project.

Summoning the chief builder, the king pointed to the arched entrance and asked, "When the supports are removed, will the stones stand?"

"Without question," the builder replied. "I shaped the keystone and laid it in place with my own hands."

When the king expressed doubt, the builder walked to the palace entrance and took his place confidently beneath the tons of stone that formed the arch.

"I will stand here while we test the arch," said the builder. "I entrust my life to the keystone."

When the laborers knocked away the timber supports, the arch held fast, and the keystone vindicated the builder's faith.

Jesus Christ is the living keystone who holds life together. Trusting him may appear risky, but the true risk is trying to build without him.

Ten

THE CARPENTER'S
TOOLBOX

My yoke is easy, and my burden is light.
—MATTHEW 11:30

The Roman era, during which Jesus practiced his craft, was a golden age of woodworking. Thanks to technological advances and innovations during the relatively peaceful reign of Rome, most of the tools available to nineteenth-century carpenters would have been familiar to Jesus. The information uncovered by archaeologists and historians allows us to make an educated guess about the implements in the toolbox of a typical Galilean carpenter of two thousand years ago.

THE RIGHT TOOL FOR THE JOB

Jesus likely had an array of bronze and iron tools for shaping wood. He had an ax for felling trees, and he and Joseph probably used a large frame saw for ripping logs into planks and boards. For more precise woodworking, Jesus relied on the adz, a kind of hatchet with the blade set horizontally. An adz was indispensable for hewing timber to a desired shape. After the adz did the heavy carving, Jesus used chisels, planes, and files for finishing. The spokeshave, a Roman invention that gave greater blade control than the more traditional chisel, was probably in use at the time.

Jesus didn't have the modern brace and bit, so he bored holes with a bow drill. The bow was a frame-and-cord arrangement that allowed the carpenter to spin a bit-tipped rod back and forth. The process was slow compared to modern power drills, but the results were precise. Archaeologists have also unearthed impressive examples of turned wood from this period, so Jesus may have used a lathe in his shop.

Jesus owned several saws, but the quality of ancient metalworking fell far short of modern standards. Iron saw blades tended to be too weak for back-and-forth motion. Pushing the saw stressed the metal beyond its limits, resulting in a bowed or broken saw. The bow saw offered one way to strengthen the saw by stretching a thin blade tightly in a frame. The tension on the blade held it taut within the frame and prevented it from buckling. Bow-saw blades were too rough for finished work, however, and the frame prevented the blade from cutting completely through a wide board or a thick beam.

The most common saw of Jesus's day was the pull saw. A metal blade was affixed to a straight wooden handle, creating a tool that looked more like a dagger or sword than a modern handsaw. Pull saws cut in only one direction. Angled teeth bit into the wood as the carpenter drew the saw toward him. After drawing the saw, the carpenter shifted the blade for another pull stroke, repeating this until he had completed the cut.

We have considered the Carpenter's responsibility to cut away knots and twisted wood from our lives. When we find ourselves in that painful situation, we might recall the pull saw Jesus used in his work. That saw never pushes the wood away from the carpenter; it always drags the wood toward him. Even when the Master Carpenter lays his saw upon our lives, he never seeks to drive us away. Every stroke is meant to draw us closer.

YOKES MADE TO ORDER

Knowing so many tools were available at the time, can we assume that Jesus was skilled in his work? Not necessarily.

Tools alone do not make a carpenter. Even so, we have scraps of evidence that Jesus excelled at his trade, particularly in shaping wood to precise specifications. Around AD 100 an early Christian named Justin wrote that Jesus was a carpenter before he began his ministry. That much we already know from the gospel of Mark, but Justin added specifically that Jesus made yokes and ploughs, using them as object lessons in his teaching.

We find one of those object lessons in the gospel of Matthew when Christ said,

> Come to me, all you that are weary and are carrying
> heavy burdens, and I will give you rest. Take my
> yoke upon you, and learn from me; for I am gentle
> and humble in heart, and you will find rest for your
> souls. For my yoke is easy, and my burden is light.
> (11:28-30)

Did Jesus mention the yoke because he was well re- spected for his skill as a yoke maker? Many scholars think so. Indeed, some suggest that the words "My yoke is easy" orig- inally served as an advertising slogan for Jesus during his car- pentry years. The idea is plausible, especially when we realize that an "easy" yoke was one that was well fitted.

If this guesswork is accurate, we learn two things about Jesus. He expertly shaped wood, adding the curves to seat a yoke precisely on the uneven neck of an ox. And he cared enough about the comfort of a beast of labor to carve a yoke that wouldn't rub the helpless ox, causing blisters and ulcers. If the Carpenter took such pains to ensure the welfare of an animal, surely he will ease the burdens of his followers.

STRAIGHT AND TRUE

The toolbox of Jesus also contained a variety of measuring tools: a rule, a line, a compass, and some kind of stylus or marking instrument. Precise measurement is essential in carpentry. "Measure twice; cut once" is the woodworker's adage. Nothing is more frustrating than cutting a board and hoisting it into place, only to discover that the wood is an inch too short.

In fact, I avoid using a rule whenever possible. I prefer to put the board in place and mark it directly. When I need a number of boards cut to the same measurements, I cut one board to serve as the pattern and use it to mark the rest.

I wonder if Jesus had the pattern board in mind when he told his disciples, "I have set you an example, that you also should do as I have done to you" (John 13:15). To gauge our lives, we must have a ruler—a standard of measurement—by which to evaluate our actions. We may look to our culture or to the lifestyle of our neighbors, but measuring ourselves by the pattern board of Jesus is the wisest choice. His actions and teachings provide an infallible standard for appraising our conduct. We may fall short of the standard, but our goal is to grow toward the "measure of the full stature of Christ" (Ephesians 4:13). Jesus is the only adequate yardstick for Christians.

We would also certainly find among Jesus's tools the indispensable square and plumb line. A square guarantees right angles and keeps boards properly aligned with one another. A plumb line—a frame containing a lead weight on a string—is the antique equivalent of the modern carpenter's level. The lead plummet always points straight down. The eye may misjudge the straightness of a wall or the lay of a piece of land, but the plumb line never lies. The plummet aims directly at the center of the earth.

When construction is square and level, the woodworker deems it "true." Carpenters have used that expression for thousands of years, as proved by a passage in Homer's *Odyssey*. No doubt Jesus learned from Joseph how to "true up" a doorjamb. Years later, when he laid down his tools and turned to preaching, Jesus prefaced his sermons and stories with the odd expression "Truly, truly." The carpenter-turned-preacher wanted his listeners to know that his words were square and on the level. The teachings of Jesus are true, aligned with God, and pointing to the heart of reality.

BENT NAILS?

Before we finish rummaging through the toolbox of Jesus, let's look at his hammer. Apparently, the Romans introduced a new kind of hammer early in the first century. Before Roman ingenuity arrived on the scene, hammers had only one function: driving nails. Roman technology increased the hammer's usefulness by adding two curved claws for pulling nails. Anyone who has ever bent a nail or fastened a board in the wrong place appreciates the value of a claw hammer.

What kind of hammer did Jesus use? Archaeology can't answer the question with certainty. Whether or not Jesus owned a claw hammer, he would have approved of the innovation. A claw hammer allows us to dismantle our blunders. Pulling nails gives us a second chance to get it right. Or a third chance.

Of all the tools the Carpenter might have used, the claw hammer best symbolizes the purpose of his coming: forgiveness for mistakes, a second chance, and the opportunity to rebuild.

Perhaps God was smiling when he arranged for the Savior and the claw hammer to arrive in the world at the same time.

Eleven

BEARING THE LOAD

I glorified you on earth by finishing the
work that you gave me to do.
—JOHN 17:4

I ron is stronger than skin. I have proof. Under my hair is a scar received years ago when I pitted my scalp against a metal pipe. To earn a few dollars, I was helping a cleanup crew clear a construction site. Most of us were teenagers, and during the inevitable clowning around, my head got in the way of a six-inch piece of pipe flying through the air toward the Dumpster. The resulting gash didn't warrant stitches, but I have the scar to remind me that I should have ducked.

Back when I did construction work, I accumulated my share of knocks and bangs. I'm thankful I never visited the emergency room. Even when I fell off a roof one day, I merely brushed myself off and climbed back up the ladder. Nicks, cuts, splinters, bruises, bloody fingers, and smashed toes are the standard badges of carpentry that woodworkers take in stride.

Mishaps are not the only cost of carpentry. The work itself is inherently demanding. Blistering sun, blowing snow, and soupy mud afflict the builder. Sawdust clings to sweat-sheened skin. Physical exertion demands its due in fatigue, sore muscles, and achy joints. Once, at the end of a long day of work, I couldn't release my grip on the hammer. With my other hand, I pried cramped fingers one by one from the hammer's handle.

Carpentry demands the best effort of eye, hand, mind, and muscle. Hammers are harder than fingers, saws chew through flesh as readily as pine, and boards are tougher than bones. However cautious carpenters are, an occasional injury is inevitable when you work at a dangerous job.

RISKY BUSINESS

One day while my dad was driving nails, a chip of steel shattered from the hammerhead and struck him in the chest like a bullet. The shard buried itself in his flesh, and the impact knocked Dad off the ladder.

At the hospital, an ER physician examined Dad's x-ray and declared him a lucky man.

"If the steel fragment had hit your heart," the doctor informed him, "we wouldn't be having this conversation."

"Is it dangerous now?" Dad asked.

"No. We'll give you antibiotics to make sure no infection sets in."

"You're going to leave it in my chest?"

"We'd just do more damage digging it out," the doctor said. "Keep it as a souvenir."

To this day Dad has a fragment of steel in his chest. My father gets into his work. And vice versa.

Power tools eliminate some of the physical labor from carpentry, but they also make the work more dangerous. A physician friend tells me that, thanks to the popularity of nail guns, his emergency room regularly admits carpenters with nails embedded in arms, chests, or even heads. One worker actually shot a nail through the roof of his mouth.

Statistically, construction work is one of the most dangerous jobs in America. Injuries are an occupational hazard when frail flesh wrestles with timber, stone, and metal. Sooner or later most carpenters contribute blood to their work.

So did Jesus, but the Master Carpenter's bloodshed was

no accident. He spilled his blood on purpose. He anointed his work with blood because that was the job he came to do. He offered his flesh to the nails because nothing less would finish the work. Like the best carpenters, Jesus poured his heart into the task. He held nothing back.

SHIFTING THE WEIGHT

While serving as a volunteer chaplain for the local police department, I was once summoned to the scene of a construction accident. A trench for sewer lines hadn't been properly shored up, and the walls of earth had collapsed, burying a worker. Frantic efforts to dig the man free came too late. The sheer mass of the clay killed him almost instantly.

Anyone who has hoisted concrete blocks or wrestled rafters into place appreciates the effort—and the risk—of properly positioning weight. Supporting heavy walls requires a solid foundation. Joists shore up the floor. Load-bearing walls carry the rafters and roof. The heavy burden of stone and timber must be laid on footers and foundations that will stand strong beneath the load. If weight is misplaced, the house will fall.

Salvaging a sagging structure is often even more difficult than building from scratch, and more dangerous as well. Broken joists and bowed beams pose a threat when they bow beneath the weight they were intended to support. No one who has felt the earth tremble beneath the slamming force of a falling brick wall can ever again be casual about the danger of weight.

God sent Jesus to earth to do the heavy lifting: to repair the structural damage inflicted by human sin. Instead of a creation of joyful harmony, a tottering world leaned perilously close to collapse. Jesus saw that the terrible weight of sin was crushing God's children. We could not stand under the weight of our mistakes, the load of guilt, and the oppression of our separation from God. To do his job—to free us for abundant life—Jesus had to lift our burden. To shift the weight somewhere else, he came up with a blueprint for salvation. The supply list was short: two beams, three nails, and a load bearer to carry the weight of sin for all humanity.

Jesus knew his job was dangerous. He thought it through, searching for an alternative, hoping for a less costly approach, but there was no other way to do the job. The nails, the crossbeams, and the Carpenter himself—the job required nothing less and needed nothing more. If the nails could bear his weight, he could carry the weight of human sin, shifting the burden from the bowed back of humanity to his strong shoulders.

Of course, Jesus could have walked away from the job. No one forced him to undertake the work. Who would blame him if he laid down his tools and refused the task? Carpenters are supposed to drive nails, not be impaled by them. Who could fault him if he returned to Nazareth, opened a handyman shop, got married, raised a family, and lived to play with his grandchildren?

But God's ultimate salvage plan was on the line. The world teetered on the brink of collapse, and the future of humanity was at stake. Jesus was the only one who could bear the soul-crushing weight of our sin, repair the damage, and restore a broken creation.

No matter the cost, the Master Carpenter refused to fail either the Father who sent him or the people who needed him. Staggering beneath the killing burden, he completed the job. He carried the load of our guilt, not because he had to, but because he chose to. "No one takes [my life] from me," he said, "but I lay it down of my own accord" (John 10:18).

THE HARDEST JOB

And so to give us a second chance, Jesus went to Jerusalem and did the tough work nobody else could do. The carpenter who had carried boards on his shoulder carried a cross to a hilltop and shouldered the weight of the world's guilt. Even as he hung there, he could have changed his mind. He had the power to answer the mockers who challenged him. He could have proved himself by coming down from the cross. But rather than lay down the weight, he carried it to the bitterest of all bitter ends.

In his final moments, when the job neared completion, did he ponder the discarded hammer at the foot of the cross, recalling carefree days of childhood spent in Joseph's carpentry shop? Did he stretch his cramping fingers to stroke the blunt nailheads pressed against his palms, giving thanks for all he had built in his brief life? When his heart broke and the last strength trickled from his tortured body, did he sigh with satisfaction to behold his final workmanship?

We cannot say. All we know is that he didn't quit. He carried the load for us, shifting the killing weight to his own bloody back. When he had carried it far enough, he lifted his face to heaven and, with his final breath, whispered, "It is finished" (John 19:30).

He was finished, too. Just one more carpenter who died doing a dangerous job.

Or so it seemed.

His friends took him down from the cross and wrapped his torn and broken body in a sheet. They carried him to a nearby garden and gently laid him to rest in a tomb. According to the custom of the day, they closed the mouth of the tomb with a great boulder. They wept as the stone rolled into place, sealing the Carpenter away from their view forever.

Then those who loved him went back to their affairs, grieving for their friend, believing he was gone for good—as if a couple of tons of limestone would stop a man who had just carried the world on his shoulders.

Twelve

REBUILDING
THE TEMPLE

Destroy this temple, and in three

days I will raise it up.

—JOHN 2:19

"How goes the renovation?" I asked when I bumped
into Scott in a coffee shop.

"It's not going at all," he told me.

Scott's grandfather, a lifelong member of my congrega-
tion, had died a few months before, and the family homestead passed into Scott's hands. He and his wife had big
plans for the antebellum home overlooking the Ohio River.

Although developers had parceled out the sprawling family acreage during the past twenty years, the original house still stood proudly among newer homes. Scott's grandfather spent more than ninety years in that house, continuing the tradition of generations.

Scott intended to raze later additions to the home, add a modern kitchen and family room, and completely replace the wiring, plumbing, and HVAC. He already owned a beautiful home, but the imposing brick homestead represented a unique piece of family history. He planned to update the old house so it could serve as a home for future generations.

"I guess you haven't driven past the house for a couple of weeks," Scott said.

"Not lately."

"You missed your chance to say good-bye," he said. "We had to tear it down."

"What happened?" I asked with genuine regret.

"Once we stripped the plaster, we found that every interior wall was constructed of a double course of brick," he explained. "Very solid, but also incredibly heavy. The whole structure was settling, and the walls were shifting out of alignment. The architects convinced us there was no cost-efficient way to salvage the house."

"What a shame," I said, recalling the pillared porch, the

high ceilings, and the majestic staircase climbing to the second floor. "You must be terribly disappointed."

Scott shrugged and spread his hands in a gesture of resignation.

"It's a loss," he agreed, "but we still own the land where generations of our family have lived and died. Our family will still be there, and we'll pass the trust along to our kids."

The Heart of Israel

To fulfill the original purpose of a building, sometimes we must tear down the old and construct something new. This poignant truth prompted Jesus to make one of his most dangerous statements.

During a visit to Jerusalem early in his ministry, Jesus indignantly drove the animal sellers and the moneychangers out of the temple courtyard. Angry Jewish leaders challenged Jesus to justify his actions, demanding proof of his authority to clear the temple.

"What sign can you show us for doing this?" they asked.

What Jesus said next reflected a carpenter's pragmatism.

"Destroy this temple," Jesus replied, "and in three days I will raise it up" (see John 2:13-22).

Jesus's answer contains more than one layer of meaning.

On one level he predicted that he would raise up the temple of his body on the third day after his crucifixion. On another level he sadly acknowledged the passing of the Jerusalem temple. The latter implication was all too clear to the Jewish priests—they would never forgive Jesus for those words.

To appreciate their anger, we must grasp the importance of the temple. King Solomon had erected the first temple one thousand years before Jesus, centralizing Jewish worship in Jerusalem. The temple was the most important building in Israel. It symbolized the presence of God among his chosen people.

That structure endured a little more than four centuries before the invading Chaldeans conquered Jerusalem and destroyed it. When the Jews returned from the Babylonian exile, they rebuilt the temple as the center of religious and national life. Resources were scarce at the time, and the second temple lacked the beauty of Solomon's opulent building.

In New Testament times, King Herod the Great undertook to correct that deficiency and initiated a massive renovation of the temple. The project began two decades before Jesus's birth and continued for more than eighty years. The resulting edifice was a wonder of the ancient world.

When Jesus audaciously declared that the temple would be destroyed again but that he could rebuild it in three days, his apparently cavalier attitude offended his enemies. At his trial, witnesses hurled the words at Jesus as an accusation, and mockers recalled his claim as he hung on the cross.

The House of God

In truth, though, Jesus loved that venerable house of God. He cherished the sanctuary hallowed by centuries of praise and prayer. He revered the glory of God revealed in its architectural grandeur.

No Jew traveled to Jerusalem without visiting the temple. The disciples of Jesus expressed typical awe when they surveyed the temple and exclaimed, "Look, Teacher, what large stones and what large buildings!" (Mark 13:1).

For many reasons the Israelites of Jesus's day could not imagine religion apart from the temple.

- God's presence and holiness dwelt there.
- The sacrifices for human sin could be offered nowhere else.
- The faithful offered their prayers and worship there.
- The temple was a refuge in desperate circumstances.
- The temple depicted God's loving covenant in stone and timber.

Jesus also recognized the temple's shortcomings, though. Surveying the temple through a carpenter's discerning eyes, Jesus knew the building needed more than the grandiose face-lift King Herod had provided. Outwardly the temple still shone in splendor, but inward spiritual decay had undermined God's fundamental intention for the structure. The day was at hand when the temple could no longer fulfill its divinely appointed purpose. The old temple must fall, and a new temple must rise in its place.

The false witnesses at his trial accused Jesus of threatening to destroy the temple. Jesus said no such thing. He did predict the fall of the temple, but he knew it would come not by his own hand but by the armies of Rome. When his disciples admired the breathtaking adornments of the temple, Jesus soberly told them, "As for these things that you see, the days will come when not one stone will be left upon another; all will be thrown down" (Luke 21:6).

That grim prophecy came to pass about thirty-five years later when Roman troops breached the defenses of Jerusalem and leveled the city, destroying the temple in the process. Today, in modern Jerusalem, the massive foundation stones of the temple's western wall are all that remain of the once-proud building.

The Romans tore the temple to the ground in AD 70. Nearly two thousand years later, the temple has never been rebuilt.

Or has it?

A New House

Christians believe that the resurrection of Jesus symbolizes the replacement of the old temple and the restoration of the temple's original purpose. The risen Christ fulfills all the temple's intended functions but has none of its shortcomings or limitations. When we review the purposes for which God called Solomon to build the original temple, we can see how the risen Christ becomes the true and eternal temple for his people.

- The fullness of God dwells in Jesus.
- Jesus's death is the sacrifice that forgives human sin once and for all.
- God receives our worship and prayers through Jesus.
- Christ is the refuge and safe haven for all who trust him.
- Jesus is God's loving covenant revealed in flesh and blood.

According to Jewish belief, God formerly dwelt behind the curtain of the temple in the Holy of Holies, aloof from ordinary mortals and unapproachable. Christians proclaim that we can enter into the throne room of God through Jesus. God is as near to us as the open arms of our Savior.

Jesus didn't destroy the physical temple, but he knew it could no longer fulfill its mission. God required a new temple not made with human hands, a place where mercy meets human need, a structure impervious to decay and open to all people.

Jesus promised to provide such a Temple and, as always, the Carpenter kept his word. He raised a new Temple to replace the old one, a Temple within reach of people everywhere, open to every race and nation, a Temple that stands forever.

The Master Carpenter built to last, and he did the job in three days flat.

Thirteen

THE HOUSE WITH MANY ROOMS

I am the door.
—JOHN 10:9, KJV

I pray Mom doesn't live much longer," Jeanette said. "When she's ready to let go, I'm ready to let her go."

Jeanette's mother had been a vibrant businesswoman—independent, energetic, and shrewd. After three years of Alzheimer's relentless onslaught, nothing remained of the woman I had known and admired. She sat all day in a wheelchair, stripped of reason, language, and relationships. When I visited, she was oblivious to my presence. I read psalms aloud to her while she compulsively picked at her sleeve or wept forlornly.

"I know a better place is waiting for her," Jeanette said. "My brothers don't understand that. They're not Christians. They have no hope for anything on the other side of death, but I do."

A PLACE PREPARED

On the night before his death, Jesus spoke words of hope to his disciples, encouraging them to face life and death without anxiety: "In my Father's house there are many dwelling places," he said. "If it were not so, would I have told you that I go to prepare a place for you?" (John 14:2).

Whatever awaits us on the other side of the grave, we will not arrive there as homeless refugees. The Carpenter is at work in the house of his Father, building a home for each of us.

During a time of expressing prayer concerns on a recent Sunday at my church, Buddy stood up from his pew near the back and said, "I have a joy to share. My mother's coming to live with us."

"Your mom's in Florida, right?" I asked.

"She and Dad retired there last year," Buddy explained,

"and Dad died just a few months later. I've finally talked her into coming back to Kentucky and moving in with us."

The following Saturday I dropped by Buddy's home to ask if he wanted some help from church members in unloading his mother's stuff when she arrived.

"Thanks," he said. "I've already got my neighbors on call. But I'm glad you're here. Let me show you the apartment we've fixed up for Mom."

He led me to the rear of the house and proudly ushered me into a spacious room with a private bath. He had installed support bars beside the toilet and the tub. I sniffed the smell of fresh paint and admired the view of the woods behind their home.

"Mom loves birds," Buddy told me. "We'll hang her feeders outside that window."

"You've put a lot of effort into this," I said.

"I hope Mom will feel at home as soon as she walks through the door," Buddy said. "I want her to have everything she needs to make her happy."

What feels better than coming home to a place where we belong, where loved ones await our arrival? When our days in this world are done, Jesus promises us a joyful homecoming. We've never visited the place that awaits us, but our hearts will be at home there. Jesus has promised it, and he will make it so.

A HOME FOR EVERY HEART

Heaven is no mass-produced neighborhood of identical cookie-cutter houses. In the infinite house of God, a unique home awaits each of us, a place prepared for us by the Carpenter.

I've known people who have labored for years to create the floor plan for a dream house. They pore over sheaves of blueprints, visit model homes, and tinker with dimensions until they have the ideal layout. Then after a few months in their perfect home, they wistfully list the things they wish they had done differently: "This room is too small. That door is in the wrong place. The patio gets too much sunlight. If only we had a coat closet by the front door."

That's why Jesus takes over the task of preparing our heavenly home. He knows us better than we know ourselves. He knows our desires and longings, even the dreams we never admit. He knows what we have sacrificed in his service. He discerns the unfulfilled possibilities slumbering in our souls. He understands what brings us joy and energizes our passion. He sees unmet needs long suppressed.

"I go to prepare a place for you," the Carpenter promises. Every home in heaven is custom-made by the Master Builder. In the Father's endless house are homes for every son and daughter. Dwelling places with southern exposures and skylights. Windows open to the sound of the sea. Poplar-paneled dining rooms and ballrooms with polished dance floors. Creek-rock fireplaces, long hallways hung with oil paintings, sunken tubs, and gazebos in azalea gardens. That's how I imagine the heavenly house with many rooms, a lovingly crafted home where no need or spiritual longing is beyond the Carpenter's ability or resources.

My grandfather, blind for most of his life, will have a bay window with a view of the sunrise over mist-shrouded mountains. And I'm sure Grandma has a big kitchen and a table that seats twenty or thirty.

My old friend Pete's heavenly home certainly has a woodworking shop with the smell of sawdust hanging in the air and curls of wood carpeting the floor.

Dr. Rhodes, my beloved seminary professor, has a whole wing for his library—complete with leather chairs, oak tables, and bright lights.

The Carpenter has built a home of many floors for my Uncle Pirtle. Climbing the stairs from room to room will thrill him after fifty years on crutches.

My friend and longtime gardening rival Bob will have a greenhouse for starting a dozen varieties of tomato plants from seed.

Of course, heaven will be far better than my imagination. We earthbound creatures can only visualize the hereafter in terms of what we have experienced in the here and now. The reality that awaits us will be infinitely richer than anything we have seen with our eyes or conjured in our fantasies.

Even earthly blueprints can be hard to follow if you're not a carpenter or an architect. The intricate drawings show the layout of rooms and the position of doors and stairways, but few people can accurately picture the final result—until they walk through the door into the finished home. We face the same problem when we talk about heaven. The Bible provides us with only a sketchy blueprint of our eternal home. We cannot know the full wonder of heaven until we arrive there.

What we do know is that Jesus promised to get a place ready for our arrival, and the Carpenter has never made a promise he hasn't kept. On the day of our homecoming, we will find a home custom-built for our joy, no room unfinished, no detail overlooked. The Carpenter, who built a world adorned with northern lights, snow crystals, and cardinals, will spare no effort or craft to build a home where we will be happy forever.

THE OPEN DOOR

Can we be sure of arriving safely in our new home? The promise of a beautiful house won't mean much if we find ourselves locked out. Can we count on Jesus to get us in?

"If I go and prepare a place for you, I will come again and will take you to myself, so that where I am, there you may be also" (John 14:3). The Carpenter will escort us in person, usher us into the handiwork he has prepared for our coming, and proudly walk us through each room, saying, "Look what I've built for you!"

On my first day at work as an ordained minister, I strolled up the church walkway with high expectations. Who knew what God might place in my hands? Maybe someone would call for spiritual guidance. A homeless person might arrive on the doorstep looking for help, or a couple might ask me to preside over their wedding. I might even receive an emergency summons from the hospital.

With butterflies in my stomach, I slipped my shiny key into the lock and attempted to open the church door. The knob fell off in my hand. I couldn't get the door open. I banged fiercely, but no one was inside to admit me. I had reported for duty, and I was locked out.

I went home, got my toolbox, came back, and opened the door. After three years of seminary education, theological training, pastoral grooming, and wrestling with Greek verbs, my first ministerial act was repairing a broken doorknob. Scarcely what I had anticipated, but in retrospect, I can't think of a better initiation to ministry. What a privilege to open the door for those who seek God.

The risen Christ undertakes the same task for his church. "These are the words of the holy one, the true one, who has the key of David, who opens and no one will shut, who shuts and no one opens.... Look, I have set before you an open door, which no one is able to shut" (Revelation 3:7-8).

The Carpenter has built a place for us in heaven. He holds the key, and he promises to open the door when we arrive. I am assured that when I come to the place prepared for me, the knob won't fall off in my hand. No one who trusts the Carpenter will be locked out. Jesus sets before us an open door.

Indeed, Jesus says, "I am the door" (John 10:9, KJV). Jesus is himself the way into God's great house. Through his love for us, through his death on the cross and his rising from the dead, he has become the door that brings us into the place prepared for us. He is the only door that leads to God.

Behind us, the Carpenter shuts the door to pain, grief, and tears. He bolts the door to regret, fear, and disappointment, and no one can open what he has locked. He opens before us a door to peace, forgiveness, and healing. He flings wide the door to God and says to us, "Enter into the joy of your master" (Matthew 25:23). Nothing can slam that door—no guilt, no failure, no doubt. If Christ unlocks a door, no power can close it.

THE OTHER SIDE

During a summer off from seminary, I bummed around Europe for a couple of months. One of the first cathedrals I saw there was the medieval church in Chartres, France. I stopped awestruck before the main entrance, the so-called Royal Portal. The twelfth-century entryway entranced me. The looming doors are framed in statuary, an overwhelming welcoming committee of prophets, kings, apostles, gospel writers, and angels. Carved over the door and reigning over all the other statues is the figure of Jesus enthroned at the end of time.

I'd never seen anything so compellingly beautiful. I studied the stone faces, deciphered the identities of biblical heroes, and traced the scenes depicting the earthly life of Jesus. I stood there on the pavement for perhaps fifteen minutes before a wizened cathedral guide padded up softly and stood respectfully at my side. After a few moments of silence, he laid a hand gently on my arm.

"Come in," he said. "If you think the door is magnificent, wait until you see what lies on the other side."

The Carpenter sets an open door before us. On the other side is not only a blissful home for eternity but also an adventure for today. Jesus is transforming the world and building renewed people to work at his side. He plans to make you the person you've dreamed of becoming, and he has work for you to share with him. Imagine what you can become in his hands and what he can accomplish through yours.

The door is open.

Wait until you see what lies on the other side.

ABOUT THE AUTHOR

H. MICHAEL BREWER is an ordained minister of the Presbyterian Church (USA) and adjunct professor of religious studies at Northern Kentucky University. He enjoys kayaks, campfires, cathedrals, and bluegrass hammers. You can learn more about his other books at *hmichaelbrewer.com.*